INSTITUTE FOR PUBLIC POLICY RESEARCH

Northern Ireland

Sharing Authority

Brendan O'Leary
Tom Lyne
Jim Marshall
Bob Rowthorn

CONTENTS

		Page
Acknowledgements		1
Chapter 1.	The Need for Fresh Thought	2
Chapter 2.	The Sources of Conflict	5
Chapter 3.	Principles of Constitutional Design	13
Chapter 4.	A Model of Shared Authority	23
Chapter 5.	The Positive Case	50
Chapter 6.	The Negative Case	84
Chapter 7.	Models of Co-Sovereignty	127
Chapter 8.	Utopianism and Realpolitik	133

Appendices A-G

A.	Sovereignty, Joint Authority and Shared Authority	136
B.	Rules for Allocating Chairs and Seats in the APNI	139
C.	The UK Subvention of Northern Ireland	145
D.	Formulae for Aid under Shared Authority	146
E.	Comparative Statistics on the Economies of Northern Ireland, the Republic and Great Britain	148
F.	Composition of GNP, Northern Ireland and Great Britain	149
G.	Main Flows of Income into Northern Ireland	150

Notes 151

Tables

5.1.	Sharing the burden	80
6.1.	Options for the Future	86
6.2.	Acceptability of Options	105
6.3.	Medium-Term Impact of Options	108

Figures

4.1.	The Executive (the SACNI)	27
4.2.	The Assembly (the APNI)	34
4.3.	Law-making	36
4.4.	The Supreme Court	39
5.1.	The Security System	72
5.2.	The Subvention	77

ACKNOWLEDGEMENTS

This text is exclusively the responsibility of the authors. We would like to thank many people who have constructively commented on draft versions. None of the following should be presumed to endorse any of our views, but every person named has improved the text through criticism or advice: Kevin McNamara MP, Amanda Francis, Professor Brian Barry, James Cornford, Dr Keith Dowding, Professor Patrick Dunleavy, Dr Conor Gearty, Dr Steven Greer, Professor Christopher Hood, Jason Kilby, Dr Chris McCrudden, Dr John McGarry, Dr Margaret Moore, Dr Marjorie Mowlam MP, Lord Prys-Davies, Bill O'Brien MP, Brendan O'Duffy, Dr Ray Richardson, Clare Short MP, Clive Soley MP, Trisha Stein, Roger Stott MP, and Dr Paul Teague. We would also like to express our gratitude to Mike Scorer of the LSE Drawing Office for putting some of our words into figures. He too bears no responsibility for our ideas.

Brendan O'Leary
Tom Lyne
Jim Marshall
Bob Rowthorn
August 1993

The Authors

Brendan O'Leary is Reader in Political Science and Public Administration at the London School of Economics. He is the author, co-author and co-editor of six books, including *The Politics of Antagonism: Understanding Northern Ireland*, *The Future of Northern Ireland*, and *The Politics of Ethnic Conflict Regulation*.
Tom Lyne has lectured at the Universities of Limerick and Portsmouth, and is the co-author and co-editor of the four volumes of *Agenda*, produced by the Irish Information Partnership. He has also written numerous articles on Irish and Northern Irish politics. He was formerly research officer to Kevin McNamara.
Jim Marshall is the Member of Parliament for Leicester South. He was shadow spokesperson on Northern Ireland during the 1987-92 parliament. He is an active member of the West European Union, for whom he has recently acted as Rapporteur, writing a paper entitled *The Future of European Security Policy*.
Bob Rowthorn is Professor of Economics, University of Cambridge, and Fellow of King's College, Cambridge. He is the author and co-author of seven books, including *Northern Ireland: The Political Economy of Conflict*.

CHAPTER 1 THE NEED FOR FRESH THOUGHT

1.1. Any fool can start a quarrel, and many fools have. To terminate a quarrel by coming to an agreement usually requires thought, patience and skill. The conflict in Northern Ireland is widely considered the least tractable problem in British and Irish politics, unamenable to reasoned statecraft. Despite the efforts of successive political leaders in Great Britain, Northern Ireland and the Republic of Ireland, no political settlement has been crafted which has resolved the region's historic antagonisms. It is even thought a mark of high intelligence to declare that 'Northern Ireland is insoluble'.

1.2. These facile 'thought-stoppers' prevent us all from examining what can be done. They make us complacent about the status quo, and allow some policy-makers to suggest that the status quo is, sadly, the best that can be had. As with Dr Pangloss after every catastrophe their assurance comes that 'all is for the best in this the best of all possible worlds'. We share a contrary perspective, lucidly expressed by Peter Robinson, MP, deputy leader of the Democratic Unionist Party:
> 'We face a situation where there is widespread instability; there are no political structures dealing with the regional government of Northern Ireland; over three thousand people have been murdered; over thirty five thousand have been maimed and mutilated. Only a fool would suggest that that was a satisfactory situation. Clearly the status quo is not acceptable.' [1]

The unacceptable nature of the status quo is also our starting point.

1.3. This report is intended as a constructive contribution to public debate in the light of a possible breakdown of the inter-party and inter-governmental talks initiated by the British and Irish governments, and the likely constitutional stalemate which might then ensue. The supposition of our analysis is that the optimal road forward for Northern Ireland lies in agreements negotiated between the political parties in Northern Ireland, the two governments and any external arbiters. However, we realise that this outcome may not occur. What we have therefore done is to think through the alternatives in the event of the inter-party talks collapsing or proving fruitless. We have aimed to design the outlines of a workable settlement.

1.4. When our original analysis was developed Northern Ireland was in political limbo: between protracted ethnic war and 'negotiation about negotiation'. Matters remain more or less unchanged today. To break this stalemate we believe that creative thinking is necessary. Our analysis unapologetically thinks big, as well as small. We aim to avoid

THE NEED FOR FRESH THOUGHT

the twin dangers of wishful thinking and pessimistic cynicism, and also the sadly all too frequent approach to Northern Ireland: not thinking at all. Creative thinking cannot come from Britocentric or Hibernocentric mythologies. Traditional interpretations of Northern Ireland must be transcended to resolve the conflict, whether they be the doctrines of nationalists and unionists, the 'common-sense' of British politicians, or the shibboleths of conservatives, Marxists, Protestants, Catholics, and atheists. However, we do not pretend that nobody has thought imaginatively or carefully about Northern Ireland. We did not start from blank pages. Instead we have attempted to build constructively upon previous analyses and proposals. We hope that our debts to other writers and analysts will be apparent.

1.5. British and Irish policy-making for Northern Ireland, with the exception of the making of the Anglo-Irish Agreement, has too often been characterised by unreflective crisis-management and resort to *ad hoc* and 'more error than trial' approaches to conflict-regulation. In defence of the two governments, and their respective civil servants, it might be said that the most obvious obstacle to understanding Northern Ireland, let alone managing it, is the fact that there is no widely agreed explanation of the conflict. There is in other words a conflict about what the conflict is about, a 'meta-conflict' [2]. However, we believe that well-formed and effective policy for Northern Ireland does not require universal consensus on the causes of conflict. That would mean permanent equivocation on policy. Provided our policy prescriptions address the interests and values held by the proponents of rival positions, and their own definitions of the causes of the conflict, we believe that the core problems of Northern Ireland can be shown to be amenable to effective resolution.

How to Read This Book

1.6. Readers who are familiar with Northern Ireland need not read Chapter 2, because the discussion within it will contain nothing that is novel for them, although the chapter does contain the essential premises of our arguments. Readers who are knowledgeable about the constitutional principles in democratic systems which have a full separation of powers or consociational practices do not need to read Chapter 3: the footnotes in Chapter 4 will guide them where necessary. Chapter 4 is essential, but the most difficult to read. It contains the institutional detail of our proposed constitutional model for Northern Ireland. In part it is deliberately written in the form of a draft constitution, but it contains some commentary and advocacy. It cannot be fully understood without an appreciation of the constitutional principles outlined in the preceding chapter, or without a reading of the argument in Chapter 5 which makes the positive case for our model of shared authority. It presents a philosophical argument for its fairness, a defence of its democratic and accountable nature, and a series of pragmatic arguments to show that a system of shared authority is compatible with a feasible system of public security and of public finance. Chapter 6, by contrast, makes the negative case for our model of shared authority, arguing that it makes greater moral, political and practical sense than any of the other major options canvassed for the future of Northern Ireland. Chapter 7 explains how our model of shared authority differs from other proposals which have suggested co-sovereignty as the best way of resolving conflict in and over Northern Ireland. Chapter 8 sums up our case. A series of appendices follow which illustrate some more technical arguments and provide information which supplements the arguments in the text.

CHAPTER 2 THE SOURCES OF CONFLICT

2.1. The conflict in and over Northern Ireland is a collective catastrophe for all the peoples of these islands. We are all affected by it, by the death and destruction it brings and by its economic, legal, security and political costs. However, the blame for the existence of the conflict and its continuation should not be exclusively or primarily laid at the door of the local peoples. Northern Ireland is the by-product of both British and Irish nation-building failures. British nation-building, from the eighteenth century onwards, failed to integrate Irish people, especially Irish Catholics, as co-nationals of the citizens of Great Britain. In part this development reflected the essentially colonial treatment of Ireland by Britain. In an equal and opposite reaction Irish nationalist movements, from the late eighteenth century onwards, failed to integrate all Irish people, especially Ulster Protestants, as co-nationals of the emergent Irish nation. The partition of Ireland in 1920, which was not inevitable, flowed from these parallel developments.

2.2. The partition of Ireland did not resolve these twin nation-building failures, and could not do so, given the heterogeneity of what became Northern Ireland, the manifest inappropriateness of the chosen border, and the nature of the political institutions within which Northern Ireland developed.[3] While there was an arguable case for the partition of Ireland there was no good case for the actual partition implemented between 1920 and 1925. The new political entity contained two peoples with a long-established history of mutual antagonism who were not integrated into either Great Britain or independent Ireland, Ulster Protestants and Irish Catholics. Moreover, the political institutions developed after 1920 in Great Britain, independent Ireland, and Northern Ireland not only failed to arrest British and Irish nation-building failures, they exaggerated them. Great Britain left Northern Ireland alone, with a miniature version of the Westminster model of government, turning a blind-eye to majoritarian political, economic and legal abuse of local power by the Ulster Unionist Party until the 1960s. The independent Irish state developed its sovereignty, constitution and public policies after 1920 at the expense of making the Irish nation attractive to Ulster Protestants, and indeed indirectly encouraged unionists to believe their political security could only be obtained by controlling the nationalist community in Northern Ireland through repression and discrimination.

2.3. The key causes of the present conflict are therefore multi-dimensional and inter-related, and must be addressed in any just and realistic settlement. Simplifying matters, the most important historic and present sources of conflict are as follows:

- Northern Ireland was created from the core of historic Ulster, which in the seventeenth century had been the site of extensive colonial plantation by Scots and English settlers. For nearly four hundred years Ulster has been culturally and religiously mixed and divided: a site of ethnic conflict and antagonism.

- Northern Ireland was created through a contested partition of Ireland, formalised in the Government of Ireland Act of 1920.

- The creation of Northern Ireland was not actively sought by either Ulster unionists or Irish nationalists. Its formation and development were the by-product of the failure of British and Irish politicians and Irish unionists and nationalists to reach a political accommodation between the 1880s and 1920.

- Northern Ireland is a site of two competing sovereignty-claims. Under §75 of the Government of Ireland Act (1920), as modified by the Ireland Act (1949) and the Northern Ireland Constitutional Acts (1973, 1974 and 1982), the British government claims unqualified sovereignty over Northern Ireland. It is the understanding of the British government that the Anglo-Irish Agreement does not qualify British sovereignty over Northern Ireland, but rather provides a mechanism through which its sovereignty might one day be changed. Under Articles 2 and 3 of the Irish Constitution (1937) the Republic of Ireland claims Northern Ireland as part of its national territory.* It is the understanding of the Irish courts that the Anglo-Irish Agreement does not qualify this claim: the re-integration of the national

---

*   This claim is a peaceful and constitutional one, similar to the constitutional clauses in the Federal Republic of Germany which anticipated the possibility of German unification. Article 29 of the Irish Constitution commits Ireland *inter alia* to 'peace and friendly co-operation amongst nations founded on international justice and morality' and 'to the principle of the pacific settlement of international disputes'. Moreover, contrary to the claims of some unionists, the Republic of Ireland's claim is neither illegal in international law, nor contrary to Ireland's adherence to the 1975 Helsinki accords (see also the note accompanying paragraph 5.12).

territory remains a constitutional imperative, the Anglo-Irish Agreement is a means towards that end.*

- Northern Ireland was developed politically in a way which intensified the historic divisions between its peoples; and its political institutions led the dominant community, unionists, who were mostly Protestants, to exercise control over the subordinate community, nationalists, who were almost entirely Catholics.

- Since its formation Northern Ireland's peoples have been divided in their national allegiances, and will remain so for the foreseeable future. National identities are not biodegradable in one generation. Presently a majority within Northern Ireland define themselves as British citizens and wish to remain in the United Kingdom, while a large and growing minority see themselves as Irish and wish to be constitutionally and institutionally linked to the Republic of Ireland.**

- Northern Ireland is a problem of both 'double minorities' and 'double majorities'. Northern nationalists are a minority in Northern Ireland, Ulster unionists are a minority within the United Kingdom, and would be a minority in a united Ireland; Irish nationalists would be a majority in a united Ireland, and Ulster unionists are a majority in Northern Ireland. Each community in Northern Ireland thinks of itself as part of a (rightful) majority, but considers itself to be an insecure and maltreated minority. In addition, across the region of Northern Ireland there are variations

---

* The Anglo-Irish Agreement was designed to make it immune to a constitutional challenge in the Irish courts. Since it could be interpreted as an agreement about how the 'national territory' could be re-integrated the Irish Supreme Court accepted its validity, while insisting that unification of Ireland was a 'constitutional imperative', a phrase which has no clear political meaning (*McGimpsey v. An Taoiseach*, 1990).

** There is therefore a fundamental bi-polar disagreement over national political identities. However, perceptions of national cultural identity are more complex: Protestants may define themselves as British, Ulsterfolk, Northern Irish or Irish - or some combination of these four categories; Catholics, by contrast, define themselves culturally as Irish or Northern Irish. In short Protestants are more likely to have two distinct identities, a British political identity and an Irish (or Northern Irish or Ulster) cultural identity, while Catholics normally do not differentiate between their political and cultural identities.

in the extent to which the two communities consider themselves local minorities or majorities. The political psychology which all these perceptions generate has negative repercussions.

- The political classes and institutions of Great Britain and the Republic of Ireland, their governments and constitutional arrangements, have both intentionally and unintentionally exacerbated conflict between their co-nationals in Northern Ireland. The clearest present examples of this phenomenon are the ambiguity of Great Britain's commitment to the maintenance of the Union, and the reciprocal ambiguity of the Republic of Ireland's commitment to Irish unification:

    - The British commitment to the Union is significantly qualified by Northern Ireland's right to secede into the Republic of Ireland on the basis of a simple popular majority, as specified in Article 1 of the Anglo-Irish Agreement.

    - The Republic's constitutional commitment to integrating Northern Ireland, specified in Articles 2 and 3 of its Constitution, is arguably not matched by other public policy actions.

    These partial commitments raise hopes in one community and fears in the other, but at the same time lack credibility, because everybody can reasonably doubt the conviction behind the declared constitutional commitments.

- There have been and there remain substantial unjustified material inequalities between the two major communities in Northern Ireland, despite over twenty years of allegedly impartial direct rule from Westminster.

    Economically, these unjustified inequalities are expressed in differential unemployment rates, levels of disposable income, housing standards, and occupational status, with the average position of those born as Catholics being systematically worse than that of those born as Protestants. [4]

    Legally, these inequalities have been expressed in differential likelihood of arrest and imprisonment under emergency legislation.

THE SOURCES OF CONFLICT

These inequalities underpin collective fears, and partially explain the existence of paramilitary violence.

- Political violence is both the consequence and cause of conflict in the region, and has self-perpetuating dynamics. Violence is partially motivated by the belief that only one side can win; it is also motivated by the belief that using it is the best way of preventing the other side from winning; and, last, but not least, it is motivated by the belief that the other side benefits from using violence so it must pay to engage in counter-violence. Northern Ireland is the most internally politically violent unit in the European Community. [5] Violence by paramilitary organizations and reciprocal state repression have created a vicious circle, undermining the prospects for democratic accommodation and the rule of law. This vicious circle will undoubtedly continue in the absence of policing and judicial institutions which are legitimate throughout both communities, and will reinforce the region's profound insecurities, hatreds and manifest prejudices.

- No purely internal settlement of Northern Ireland is possible, not only because the politics of the region are shaped by the governments and politics of Great Britain and the Republic of Ireland, but also because a crucial part of the identity of unionists and nationalists is their relations with the state with which they wish to be associated. Northern Ireland is the result of the historic stalemate between British and Irish nationalism. The British and Irish dimensions of the conflict must be recognised and reconciled in its resolution. Equally, however, no purely external settlement can be successful. The British and Irish governments must design institutions which the internal parties in Northern Ireland can come to see as viable ways of protecting their core values and interests.

2.4. We believe it follows that any successful settlement must address or accommodate

- the relationships between Northern Ireland and Great Britain and between Northern Ireland and the Republic of Ireland, the 'patron-states' of the two peoples of the region;

- the historically entrenched national, cultural and religious differences within Northern Ireland;

- the need for widely legitimate judicial and policing institutions;

- the need for a settlement which will eventually diminish the rationales for paramilitary violence; and

- the material and unjustified inequalities in Northern Ireland.

Our proposals, elaborated especially in Chapter 4, address all of these issues in some depth - with the exception of material and unjustified inequalities in Northern Ireland. These inequalities must be rectified if any settlement is to be successful in the medium to long term, but we have not extensively discussed the mechanisms which are necessary to achieve this goal - though we believe that there should be constitutional recognition of the problem (see paragraph 4. 16. 2.). [6]

2.5. In our judgement nationality is the fundamental axis of conflict in Northern Ireland. It is true that it is not the only axis of conflict. It is true that not everybody within Northern Ireland falls into the unionist or nationalist camps. * It is conceivable that Catholics are less wholeheartedly committed to separatist nationalism than Protestants are to unionist integrationism, and it may be true that not everybody who is a nationalist or a unionist is uncompromisingly so, but the national conflict is nevertheless the primary one. The national question motivates republican and loyalist paramilitaries. The national question accounts for the major cleavage between the dominant political party blocs in Northern Ireland: the unionist bloc and the nationalist bloc. It is the national question which has politically polarised the communities since 1969. Therefore the national question must be addressed squarely by any politicians or peace-makers intent

---

* As survey data often show - see e.g. John Curtice and Anthony Gallagher 'The Northern Irish Dimension' in *British Social Attitudes: the 7th Report* (Aldershot: Gower, 1990), pp. 183-216. However, scepticism is in order about polling evidence which suggests that the two peoples of Northern Ireland are more moderate in their respective forms of national extremism than their voting and militaristic behaviour suggests. As the most authoritative surveyor of research of the region declared 'In Northern Ireland people try to sound more moderate than they really feel in replying to interviewers. I would suspect, then, that the proportion of Protestants who hanker after majority rule, and of Catholics who want a united Ireland, is higher than the survey evidence indicates, and that the proportion of Catholics who would accept integration with Britain, or of both communities who would settle for power-sharing, is lower than the data suggest' (John Whyte, *Interpreting Northern Ireland* (Oxford: Clarendon Press, 1990), pp. 82-3).

THE SOURCES OF CONFLICT 11

on successful conflict-resolution. We believe that the only way in which the national question can be effectively, durably and equitably addressed is through the design of political institutions for Northern Ireland which allow authority, power and responsibility to be shared between the peoples of Northern Ireland and the governments of the United Kingdom and the Republic of Ireland.

2.6. We must emphasise the fact that two states claim sovereignty over Northern Ireland and that each of the two national communities in Northern Ireland supports one of these claims to sovereignty. The United Kingdom exercises *de facto* sovereignty over Northern Ireland, as it has done since the creation of the region in 1920. The United Kingdom's constitutional claim to Northern Ireland, insofar as one can speak of a UK constitution, has been successively expressed in the Government of Ireland Act of 1920, the Ireland Act of 1949, and in the Northern Ireland Constitution Acts (1973, 1974 and 1982). The Republic of Ireland claims sovereignty over the region in its Constitution (*Bunreacht na hEireann*, 1937: Articles 2 and 3). In 1985 the governments of the United Kingdom and the Republic of Ireland signed an international treaty, popularly known as the Anglo-Irish Agreement.* Neither state abandoned its constitutional claim to Northern Ireland, but they did agree in Article 1 that Northern Ireland's constitutional status could not be changed without the approval of a majority of the population of Northern Ireland. However, this agreement was an agreement about how Northern Ireland's constitutional status could be changed: it was not an agreement about its constitutional status. Resolving Northern Ireland manifestly requires both governments to agree on Northern Ireland's constitutional status. *The sanest solution to resolving Northern Ireland's constitutional status is for both governments to recognise that Northern Ireland is a constitutionally exceptional part of both the United Kingdom and the Republic of Ireland. In plain words both governments should recognise the validity of each other's constitutional claim.* This step, however, would merely be the first of many required to build a stable and just settlement. It requires the British and Irish governments and the peoples of Northern Ireland to break with the dogma of indivisible sovereignty.

2.7. No attempt at conflict-resolution can be justified which entails one national community triumphing at the expense of the other, either

---

* Any new agreement along the lines of what we propose below should be called the British-Irish Agreement or the Irish-British Agreement.

now or in the long-run. For this reason most of the standard options canvassed by partisan unionists must be ruled out, such as full and permanent integration of Northern Ireland into the United Kingdom, or devolution within a purely UK context. The evidence manifestly suggests that Northern Ireland cannot be legitimate and stable and democratic if it is solely British. We should all have learnt that much since 1969. However, on the same logic the options canvassed by hard-line nationalists or republicans must be ruled out, such as the full integration of Northern Ireland into the Republic of Ireland, or a federal or confederal Ireland.* Northern Ireland cannot be legitimately, democratically or stably eased into purely Irish institutions. Instead of wholly endorsing either nationalism, any British and any Irish government should advocate reconciling the different interests at stake through institutions which share political power between the two sovereign governments and the peoples of Northern Ireland. Only such a system of *shared authority* can break the present impasse and create durable and effective government.

2.8. Politics in Northern Ireland has often been described as a zero-sum game: what one community gains must be at the expense of the other. We cannot stress enough that the present political and constitutional arrangements perpetuate this state of affairs. Each new development, however seemingly insignificant, is seen by some as a step in the grand conflict over Northern Ireland's status, and so is viewed with suspicion by one side or the other, or indeed both. However, this state of affairs is also sustained by the conventional thinking, shared by many people in these islands, which insists *either* that for each nation there must be one state, *or* that for each state there must be one nation, or one dominant nation. We believe that it is possible to by-pass this conventional thinking.

---

* There are many other reasons why these options are neither desirable nor feasible, and we elaborate on them in Chapter 6. Other options, which some have proposed as fair and workable settlements, namely repartition and an independent Northern Ireland must be ruled out for similar reasons (see Chapter 6).

CHAPTER 3 PRINCIPLES OF CONSTITUTIONAL DESIGN

3.1. Northern Ireland has been and is a constitutional failure. It has never enjoyed widespread political legitimacy. In our judgement it has been a failure partly because its constitutional design before 1972 was excessively parliamentary, politically majoritarian and culturally imbalanced. These constitutional features precluded successful conflict-regulation in a territory in which there were two strong national communities with well developed historic identities, values and interests. However, not all democracies need be excessively parliamentarian, politically majoritarian and culturally imbalanced. Under any successful settlement Northern Ireland evidently requires better democratic design 7, which in turn requires the explicit use of constitutional principles mostly foreign to British and Irish governmental practice.* These principles in our judgement must include a formal *separation of powers* accompanied by *checks and balances,* and furthermore what political scientists call *consensual* and *consociational principles* of co-operative government. However, these principles will not be sufficient to derive a workable constitutional settlement; we believe that requires that Northern Ireland should also become a condominium, i.e. a political entity characterised by shared sovereignty. We must show that such a condominium can be organised according to consensual principles and with a separation of powers; and organised democratically, allowing the peoples of Northern Ireland to enjoy self-government of a kind not dissimilar to that enjoyed by the constituent components of confederations or federations.

---

* There are some important exceptions to this remark: the Republic of Ireland has many of the elements of a modern Bill of Rights embedded in Article 40 of its Constitution (although other elements of this Constitution are hardly generous to the values and interests of Ulster Protestants), and it employs a proportional representation electoral system, STV (although before the 1980s this system did not prevent long periods of majoritarian and one party dominance); the United Kingdom has introduced STV for local government, assembly and European elections in Northern Ireland; and, more significantly, both states, as members of the European Union, now have twenty years of experience as participants in institutions in which sovereignty is pooled and shared, in which simple majoritarian principles do not operate, and in which the European parliament is not the dominant locus of power and legitimacy.

Parliamentarianism and majoritarianism and their defects in nationally divided regions

3.2. In parliamentary democracies like the United Kingdom and the Republic of Ireland the legislature is the most important political body. In the United Kingdom parliament is sovereign, or, more strictly, the Crown-in-Parliament, while in the Republic of Ireland the functioning of the Oireachtas is formally constitutionally limited, and sovereignty technically rests with the people. In both countries, however, the legislature formally controls the executive because prime ministerial and cabinet authority ultimately rest on the support of the elected MPs or TDs. While there is some separation of powers in the United Kingdom and the Republic of Ireland, because of the separate existence of an executive, legislature and judiciary, both countries are fundamentally parliamentary and majoritarian, although the Republic's Supreme Court, with its power of constitutional review, has much greater autonomy than its British counterpart.

3.3. The parliamentary and majoritarian nature of democracy in the United Kingdom is easy to understand. The Westminster model of government could almost have been designed to facilitate rule by a majority of the people. Historically it has had nine key features [8]:

- a concentration of executive power, normally through one-party government, and cabinets which are based on a bare majority of legislative support;

- a fusion of executive and legislative power, because the cabinet is technically a committee of the legislature, but with practical predominance in the making of law and public policy;

- weak bicameralism, that is a two-chamber parliament in which the second chamber, the House of Lords, is not powerful;

- a predominantly two party system, both in electoral support and parliamentary representation;

- a system of party competition organised principally around one political cleavage, i.e. left and right divisions over economic policy and the distribution of income and wealth;

- an electoral system, simple plurality rule, which awards parliamentary seats to the candidates winning the most votes in single member constituencies;

- a system of unitary and centralised government, in which local governments can be abolished by the central parliament;

- an uncodified constitution with a formally minimal judicial role in interpreting 'constitutional' law; and

- an exclusively representative democracy in which the use of the referendum is unusual.

Ideally the Westminster system can be seen to give power to an electoral majority (in practice a plurality) and to facilitate strong and responsible government; strong, because the single party dominated cabinet should facilitate unity of purpose, and responsible, because the government will be held to account by the electorate for its actions.

3.4. The Republic of Ireland in its constitutional evolution has inherited many of the features of the Westminster model - although its proportional representation election system, its formal constitution, its provisions for referenda on constitutional change, and its more developed multi-party system make its democratic system less overtly parliamentarian and majoritarian than its British counterpart.

3.5. Parliamentary and majoritarian systems provide one defensible and workable model of democracy. However, they only work well in relatively homogeneous societies (or societies with a uniform national political culture in which it makes sense to think of politics shaped by the suppositions of liberal individualism). In other words they work in societies in which there is a genuine likelihood that today's minority will become tomorrow's majority or plurality, i.e. where there is effective political competition for electoral support amongst individual citizens so that the principles of responsible government can work as intended. In Great Britain and the Republic of Ireland these conditions, with qualifications, have been present for much of the twentieth century, and consequently their parliamentary and largely majoritarian democratic systems have arguably served their peoples satisfactorily.*
However, in societies profoundly divided by nationality, ethnicity, race, language or religion, i.e. bi-cultural or multi-cultural societies, simple parliamentary and majoritarian democratic systems are not likely to win widespread legitimacy, and the suppositions of liberal

---

* Naturally we should not be read as providing an unqualified endorsement of the democracies of Great Britain and the Republic of Ireland. However, we do not deny that these systems enjoyed very considerable and widespread legitimacy between the 1930s and 1970s.

individualism can be usurped by a dominant community to advance its own exclusive interests. In such circumstances the institutions of parliamentarianism and majority rule are very likely to become instruments of tyranny for the largest or majority community. That is, to put matters briefly, what occurred in Northern Ireland between 1920 and 1972, when the region had its own miniature version of the Westminster model of government imposed under the Government of Ireland Act. In these years the Ulster Unionist Party won all the local parliamentary elections, and during this half century of one party rule it presided over a system of institutionalised political, economic and cultural discrimination. For these reasons Northern Ireland is now widely regarded as a textbook example of the deficiencies of the Westminster model in heterogeneous societies. The textbooks are right. To become a viable and functioning democratic entity Northern Ireland requires principles of constitutional design which recognise its bi-cultural realties. It requires a departure from the Westminster model.

Consensual and consociational constitutional principles

3.6. The logical antonym of parliamentary majoritarianism is the consensual model of democracy, which, in principle, seeks to maximise the extent of participation and representation in government, and to provide restraints on the degree to which a majority or powerful plurality can exercise governmental power. Whereas the majoritarian model defines the people who are to rule in a democracy as 'the majority', the consensual model defines it as 'as many people as possible'. Consensual democracy, as its name suggests, is much more appropriate for culturally divided societies, and much more likely to inhibit dominance, and insurrection against such dominance. In consensual democratic systems eight key institutional features can be identified (many of which are found in the Swiss system of governance):

- executive power-sharing, so that 'over-sized' and in some cases 'grand coalition' governments are formed which enjoy widespread support within and across the multiple communities which make up the democratic system;

- a separation of powers, both formal and informal, i.e. a system in which the executive is more or less invulnerable to legislative attack;

- balanced bicameralism, in which there are two chambers of parliament, and special care is taken to ensure that minority and territorial representation are established in the second chamber;

PRINCIPLES OF CONSTITUTIONAL DESIGN 17

- a multi-party system which reflects the multi-cultural nature of the constituent societies;

- a multi-dimensional party system in which non socio-economic cleavages are electorally expressed and informally institutionalised in support for political parties;

- a proportional representation voting system which ensures that the elected chambers are broadly representative of the electorate;

- a form of decentralisation which may contain both territorial and non-territorial elements, which may include explicitly federal forms, but which allows cultural communities considerable self-government - for example in the field of education; and

- a formal codified constitution which provides minorities with specific constitutional protections and rights of veto.

3.7. Consensual constitutional principles of democracy are non-exclusionary. They aim to ensure that all those affected by decisions should have institutional opportunities to participate in decisions which affect them, either directly or through their elected representatives. They also favour cultural autonomy: they aim to ensure that communities are allowed considerable institutional opportunities to govern themselves provided that they respect the same rights for others. We draw extensively upon most of the eight elements of the consensual model of democracy in our proposals for shared authority outlined in Chapter 4. We have designed an executive which guarantees the creation of a multi-member and multi-party executive; suggested a formal separation of powers between executive, legislature and judiciary; proposed a representative assembly for Northern Ireland and appropriate representation for Northern Ireland in the second chambers of Great Britain and the Republic of Ireland; recommended proportional representation electoral rules and proportionality rules for the formation of committees in the Northern Ireland assembly; endorsed non-territorial autonomy for religious and national communities and associations; and outlined the elements of a codified constitution which provides safeguards and protections for the present minority (northern nationalists) and for a possible future minority (Ulster unionists). The model we have designed assumes, reasonably, that Northern Ireland will continue to have a multi-party system, and we hope, reasonably, that if the system we have outlined is established and operated that electoral competition will become more multi-dimensional because of our proposals for resolving the national question.

3.8. The consensual model of democratic government is similar, but not identical with the elements of consociational democracy identified by the Dutch political scientist Arend Lijphart.[9] He believes, in our view correctly, that consociational systems have a proven, though far from perfect, record in regulating ethnic, linguistic and religious conflicts and divisions in bi-cultural and multi-cultural societies. Consociational systems have four defining features: (i) power-sharing between communities; (ii) proportional representation rules and proportional allocational rules; (iii) community autonomy norms, and (iv) constitutional safeguards and veto rights for minorities. In all these respects (power-sharing, proportionality, community autonomy and constitutional safeguards) the proposals we outline in Chapter 4 are consociational in character.

3.9. However, we recognise that consociational principles have often failed to work in nationally and ethnically divided societies. It is for this reason that we believe that consociational practices need to be supplemented by a practical resolution of the key source of national and ethnic division: the status of Northern Ireland. Our consociational proposals are therefore elaborated within a framework of shared authority, in which the governments of Great Britain and the Republic of Ireland share authority, power and responsibility with the peoples of Northern Ireland. We propose to resolve the national question by guaranteeing both sides full and durable protection of their national identity and their status as citizens of their preferred state. With both national traditions established on a fully equal footing we believe it will be easier for consensual and consociational practices to take root.

3.10. We also recognise that consociation has often failed to work where it requires an entirely voluntary agreement between political parties within a legislature to share executive power, an agreement which might easily be broken by the withdrawal of legislative support, or the departure of a key political party from a coalition within a purely parliamentary system. One solution to this fundamental problem is to have an executive which need not require a formal coalition between political parties, and need not rest on legislative or parliamentary support. We believe, in other words, that consociation can work with a separation of powers - including what is tantamount to the creation of a multi-person presidency. Opposition to the institution of presidentialism in nationally and ethnically divided societies has been based on the idea that presidentialism is necessarily majoritarian, but that is so only if presidentialism requires a single

PRINCIPLES OF CONSTITUTIONAL DESIGN 19

president. We propose in Chapter 4 a multi-person executive, which may be considered a multi-person presidency, which will only be required to be unanimous in proposing legislation which is deemed fundamentally to affect national and religious rights and freedoms.

Separating Powers and Checks and Balances

3.11. Controlling governmental action lies at the heart of much constitutional thought.[10] The separation of powers is the classic device invented in early modern political theory to attempt to ensure constitutionalism. The pure doctrine, which might be taken to imply that the executive, the legislature and the judiciary should divide up governmental functions in such a manner that the different branches of government need never exercise the functions of another, is, of course, entirely implausible. Rules are made by legislatures, judges, and by bureaucrats working for the executive; rules are applied by courts as well as by the executive; and judgements are made by civil servants and ministers as well as by judges. However, under a sensible interpretation of the doctrine of the separation of powers, governmental power and authority - executive, legislative and judicial - are institutionally separated but enabled to co-operate together within a constitutional framework which limits and balances the individual capacities of each branch of government.

3.12. We are persuaded of the merits of a more formal separation of powers for Northern Ireland's institutions than exists at present. This classical device will further assist in preventing the concentration of governmental power, which has been a major cause of antagonism in Northern Ireland, both in the past and at present. For this reason we propose an executive which will be independent of a Northern Ireland assembly, with the ability to propose laws subject to appropriate passage (and possible amendments) through an assembly. This executive, because it will be independent of the legislature will be stable, much more stable than, for instance, the voluntary power-sharing executive formed by Brian Faulkner, Gerry Fitt and Oliver Napier, the leaders of the Ulster Unionist, Social Democratic and Labour and Alliance parties in 1974. Good government requires a capable executive, and for that reason we propose a powerful executive. Precisely because of its potential power we believe that the executive must be a multi-person body rather than a single person president; the executive must also be structured in such a way that it cannot easily become an instrument of dominance by a permanent majority. Consequently we have proposed that the executive can only be very powerful where it is unanimous in making legislative proposals on matters fundamentally affecting national and religious rights and freedoms. We have not, however, handicapped its capacity to propose ordinary public policy measures through majority rule. To ensure the absence of a permanent majority within the executive we have also proposed that a five person executive be established, consisting of two elected representatives who are ministers of the British and Irish parliaments, and three persons directly elected by the population of Northern Ireland. This arrangement will ensure that the executive contains members from both the British and Irish parliaments, and members elected by the electorate of Northern Ireland. On such an executive we see no reason to believe why there should be a permanent political majority on matters of non-national and non-religious public policy. Political alternation in Great Britain and the Republic, and conceivably also in Northern Ireland, should ensure regular changes in the ideological orientations of members of the executive.

3.13. A formal separation of powers and a formal constitution presuppose a formal role for judicial review and interpretation of the constitution. Despite the risks inherent in the 'legalisation of politics', what some refer to as 'juridification', we believe that provided that judges are representative there is a creative and protective role for them to play in establishing workable democratic institutions in Northern Ireland. An autonomous judiciary can considerably assist in supporting the rule of law and in protecting individual and collective cultural rights specified in our outlined Constitution. We have accepted the arguments that certain rights, for all the difficulties that arise in their interpretation, must be constitutionally and judicially protected against possible majoritarian abuses. However, we also recognise that because judges of the Supreme Court of Northern Ireland will play a pivotal role in supervising the Constitution of Northern Ireland proposals are required to facilitate the formation of a Supreme Court which will be representative of Northern Ireland's communities and its condominial status. We have also taken care to consider other features of the legal system and the administration of justice in Northern Ireland which need to be re-designed to be compatible with consociational and consensual principles of democracy.

Constitutional Principles and a Democratic Condominium

3.14. Lastly, for reasons we advance particularly in Chapters 5 and 6, we believe that a successful settlement of Northern Ireland requires that it be established under international law, British public law and Irish constitutional law, as a condominium with an autonomous legal

PRINCIPLES OF CONSTITUTIONAL DESIGN 21

personality. The details are outlined in Chapter 4. What we need to explain here are the constitutional principles used in designing our model of a condominium. Our point of departure was to seek an equal and fair solution to the national question in Northern Ireland. We realised that condominia are not unknown to international law. Many condominia have existed in medieval and modern times, from the Sudan to the New Hebrides. Some condominia have been amazingly durable, like that of Andorra, which was subject to the sovereignty of the Bishop of Navarre and the ruler of France for over 700 years. Historically, however, we realise there have been types of shared sovereignty in which there has been a dominant partner. Yet, we believe that a condominium, properly construed, is a case of sovereignty jointly exercised by two or more states on a basis of equality. For this reason we have ensured that the model outlined in Chapter 4 ensures full equality of status for the United Kingdom and the Republic of Ireland with regard to Northern Ireland. We also realise that many condominia have been colonial, with external powers jointly dominating a subordinated territory and its constituent peoples. We do not propose that Northern Ireland should be made a joint colony of the United Kingdom and the Republic of Ireland. Rather we have proposed institutions which will maximise the autonomy and self-government of the peoples of Northern Ireland. We believe that these institutions will ensure that Northern Ireland is a recognisably democratic condominium, rather than a colony.

3.15. The procedural criteria for establishing a modern democracy have been identified by Robert Dahl, who has argued that a responsive democracy can exist only if at least eight institutional guarantees are present: (i) freedom to form and join political organisations; (ii) freedom of expression; (iii) the right to vote; (iv) free and fair elections (v) eligibility of adults for public office; (vi) the right of political leaders to compete for support and votes; (vii) multiple sources of information; and (viii) institutions for making public policies which depend on votes and other expressions of preference.[11] The model we outline in Chapter 4 satisfies these institutional criteria. The normal civil liberties, a free and fair electoral system, and freedom of political expression, association and competition are built into our model. The assembly and a majority of the executive will be elected by the peoples of Northern Ireland, who will also, on our proposals, elect representatives to reformed second chambers in Great Britain and the Republic of Ireland. The British and Irish members of the executive will represent the national preferences of the two national communities in Northern Ireland. They will also represent the quasi-federal relationships between Northern Ireland, Great Britain and the Republic of Ireland. We have also defined the constitutional status of Northern

Ireland to satisfy the reasonable preferences of both national communities, and have left open to the peoples of Northern Ireland ways to change the status of Northern Ireland and its constitution - provided such changes can achieve very widespread consent.

3.16. Having outlined the constitutional principles which inform our thinking we are now in a position to present our model in considerable institutional detail. Naturally there are other conceivable models which would be consistent with our constitutional principles, but we must emphasise that it is in the spirit of consensual democracy, and consociational liberal constitutionalism that we put forward our model for public debate and argument. Having outlined the details of our model in Chapter 4 we proceed to defend it positively in Chapter 5. Then we show why it is better than other ways which have been proposed for resolving Northern Ireland in Chapter 6. Finally, we distinguish our model from other condominial proposals in Chapter 7.

CHAPTER 4   A MODEL OF SHARED AUTHORITY

4.1. We outline here an institutional framework for the development of shared authority, responsibility and power, which for brevity's sake we shall refer to throughout as shared authority. It is designed to share authority, responsibility and power between the British and Irish governments, the peoples of Northern Ireland and their political institutions. A crucial feature of the model is its inter-locking nature. Another is that it does not correspond to any model of political and constitutional institutions as traditionally understood either in the Republic of Ireland or the United Kingdom. If people insist on giving our model of shared authority a simple technical name, what is proposed can be described as a democratised and autonomous condominium.* The democratic structures of the proposed condominium include a collective executive, a separation of executive, legislative and judicial powers, and a system of checks and balances. The autonomous nature of the condominium is reflected in its capacity for self-government and its capacity to obtain more autonomy with the broad consent of its peoples. Its condominial nature is reflected in the fact that the United Kingdom and the Republic of Ireland are the external co-sovereigns of the region.

4.2. Any coherent and acceptable system of shared authority established over and within Northern Ireland must satisfy the following conditions:

- In an international treaty, establishing the Constitution of Northern Ireland, it must be made plain that Britain and the Republic of Ireland are external co-sovereigns of the region, and have resolved their conflicting claims;

- Before coming into force the said international treaty must be subject to the ratification of the Westminster Parliament and to Westminster legislation to give effect to the provisions of the treaty in Britain and Northern Ireland; and it would also be subject to a motion of approval in Dáil Éireann pending the passage of an appropriate constitutional amendment in the Republic of Ireland through a popular referendum;

---

*   More precisely it is a democratised autonomous condominium which combines consociational democratic institutions with a separation-of-powers regime (See Chapter 3).

- The international treaty establishing the Constitution of Northern Ireland should incorporate the European Convention on Human Rights and other protections of fundamental freedoms into the domestic law of Northern Ireland;

- The Constitution of Northern Ireland must be subject to judicial review by the Supreme Court of Northern Ireland, whose decisions may be appealed to the European Court of Justice and the European Court of Human Rights *;

- The international treaty establishing shared authority and the Constitution of Northern Ireland must be subject to the provisions of the Treaty of Rome, the Single European Act, and the European Union;

- The citizens of Northern Ireland must be free to choose to enjoy British, or Irish, or dual citizenship rights, and enjoy full citizenship rights, including voting rights, if resident in any of the three jurisdictions of Great Britain, the Republic of Ireland and Northern Ireland;

- Northern Ireland shall have two heads of state, the Monarch of the United Kingdom, and the President of Ireland; and

- The national insignia and national cultures of both Britain and Ireland shall be fully and equally respected in the government of Northern Ireland.

Our model of shared authority presupposes the preceding ingredients.

The Status of Northern Ireland

4.3. We believe that Article 1 of the Constitution of Northern Ireland should be worded as follows:
'Northern Ireland is an autonomous and democratic political region, part of the national territory of the United Kingdom and the Republic of Ireland. Its sovereignty is vested in its peoples and their respective states who are the guardians and guarantors of its Constitution. Its citizens are entitled to full citizenship

---

* To permit direct legal appeals by aggrieved parties to the European Courts of Justice and Human Rights would require amendments to the Treaty of Rome and the European Convention on Human Rights.

rights of either the Republic of Ireland or the United Kingdom, or both. Its government is organised according to co-operative principles, which guarantee the rights and fundamental freedoms of its constituent nationalities and religions, ensure the proportional representation of its constituent communities in public institutions, and protects their equality and security'. *
Consistent with the presuppositions of our proposed Article 1 of the Constitution of Northern Ireland our model proposes three essential layers of government :

- the Shared Authority Council of Northern Ireland (SACNI);
- the Assembly of the Peoples of Northern Ireland (APNI); and
- the Supreme Court of the Peoples of Northern Ireland.

The Shared Authority Council of Northern Ireland (SACNI)

4.4. The apex of shared authority will be the Shared Authority Council of Northern Ireland, established under the terms of the Treaty which defines and incorporates Northern Ireland's Constitution - see Figure 4.1. It may be considered the supreme executive authority for Northern Ireland, although it will possess both executive and legislative powers.** The SACNI will also propose the budget for Northern

---

* This Article defines Northern Ireland's dual national status and its external co-sovereigns. The specific reference to the democratic nature of Northern Ireland's constitution is designed to give guidance to the judges of Northern Ireland's Supreme Court, who need to know the foundational principles for interpreting the constitution. The specific reference to 'co-operative principles' of government, and their elucidation, is designed to signal to the judges the consociational nature of the political institutions, and to encourage them to balance both consociational and democratic principles in their decision-making (see Chapter 3). Article 1 shall be qualified by the articles proposed in paragraph 4.16 below, which shall prevent the judiciary from finding unconstitutional public policies which are designed to promote affirmative action and substantive equality.
** This feature is no constitutional oddity. The executive in presidential systems has important legislative powers, albeit more in some regimes than others; and in parliamentary regimes lawmaking often takes place within the cabinet rather than on the floor of an assembly (See *inter alia* Matthew Soberg Shugart and John M. Carey *Presidents and Assemblies: Constitutional Design and Electoral Dynamics,* Cambridge, Cambridge University Press, 1992). It may therefore help readers to think of the SACNI as a special multi-person

Ireland, after negotiations with the British Treasury and the Irish Ministry of Finance. In the event of a breakdown of the functioning of other political institutions the SACNI will possess emergency executive authority.

    4.4.1. The SACNI will consist of five members, jointly appointed by the heads of state of Great Britain and the Republic of Ireland.* It will comprise three members elected by the peoples of Northern Ireland, one member of the House of Commons, representing a constituency in Great Britain, nominated by the Prime Minister, and one member of Dáil Éireann, representing a constituency in the Republic of Ireland, nominated by the Taoiseach. Explicit constitutional conventions will operate requiring the heads of state to appoint to the Council the nominees of the British and Irish heads of government and the three successful candidates in the Northern Ireland election.

    4.4.2. The three members representing the peoples of Northern Ireland will be elected for four years by a proportional representation voting system, with Northern Ireland treated as a single constituency.** They will therefore be accountable to the local electorate for their conduct of office. The Northern Ireland members must be willing to operate the Constitution of Northern Ireland. They will not normally be subject to removal prior to the termination of their four year period of office,*** but their valid nomination papers will include a list of three ranked substitutes to replace successful candidates in the event of their death or resignation; the top-ranked replacement will be drawn from the

---

presidency rather than the kind of executive associated with traditional UK and Irish government.

* It would be consistent with the spirit of shared authority that the Monarch shall continue to be described as the Queen (or King) of Great Britain and Northern Ireland, while the President of Ireland is described as the President of Ireland and Northern Ireland.

** The system of STV(PR), presently employed for the election of Members of the European Parliament, should be the system of proportional representation used to choose the three directly elected members of the SACNI.

*** In other words they cannot be dismissed from office by the heads of state, other than (a) under the emergency provisions specified in 4. 25 below, or (b) because of conviction of a 'serious arrestable offence' which shall be legally defined along the lines of section 116 of the *Police and Criminal Evidence Act* (1984).

A MODEL OF SHARED AUTHORITY

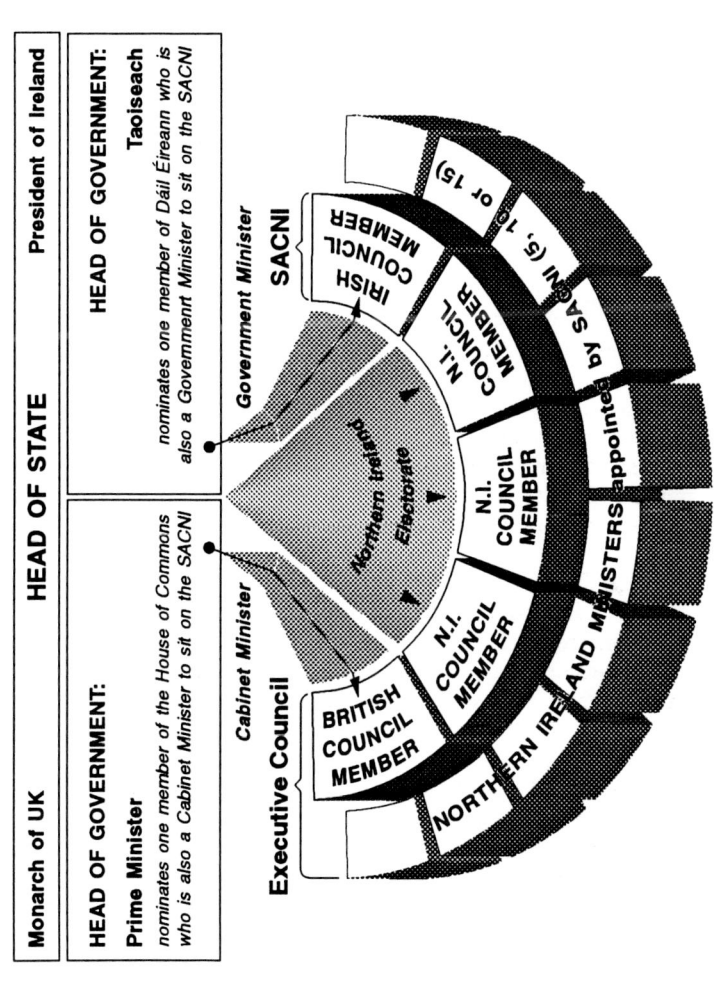

Figure 4.1

same list as the person whose demise or resignation created a vacancy.

4.4.3. The nominees of the two governments will also be ministers in the British Cabinet and in the Irish Government.* Their terms of office must coincide with that of the governments which nominate them, unless they tender their resignations or are dismissed by the relevant prime minister.** They will be appointed with deputies of junior ministerial rank.***

4.4.4. The nominated members will be responsible to their respective legislatures, the member from Great Britain answering questions in the House of Commons and his or her deputy answering questions in the Lords (or its successor), the member from the Republic and his or her deputy doing likewise in Dáil Éireann and the Senate. In the interests of democratic legitimacy and accountability the Treaty establishing Northern Ireland's Constitution will have to make provision for appropriate representation for the peoples of Northern Ireland in the Westminster and Leinster House parliaments. This change will require appropriate amendments of the Irish Constitution and the Representation of the People Act in Great Britain.****

---

* The Irish Constitution describes as 'the Government' what in the UK is referred to as 'the Cabinet'. We respect this usage throughout.
** There is an argument for enhancing the independence of the nominated members, by making them subject to removal only by a vote of the relevant legislature (Westminster or Dáil Éireann). However, the political and security responsibilities of heads of government would make it practically impossible for the nominated members to function without the full confidence of their respective head of government.
*** These deputies will not be entitled to vote in the SACNI. For the reasons given in the following footnote we believe that the British deputy should be drawn from the House of Lords (or its successor).
**** We believe that the most appropriate representation for Northern Ireland members would be in reformed second chambers in Great Britain and the Republic of Ireland. The Irish Senate and the reformed British House of Lords could be re-modelled to ensure that they are vehicles in which territorial representation of local governments and regions are crucial, and that they are forums with special responsibility for safeguarding human rights and constitutional freedoms. Our ideas for appropriate representation of Northern Ireland in the two legislatures are therefore consistent with feasible proposals

A MODEL OF SHARED AUTHORITY

4.4.5. The members of the SACNI shall therefore be held accountable in different ways. The three Northern Irish members will be directly accountable to their electorate, while the British and Irish members will be directly accountable to their respective legislatures and heads of government. In such circumstances no effectively binding legal or constitutional requirement for cabinet-style collective responsibility can operate - beyond that of a binding requirement not to disclose information jeopardising the security of these islands. The SACNI therefore cannot nor should it operate according to collective responsibility as understood in the constitutional practice of these islands.* We believe, however, that the necessities of working together will produce acceptable forms of solidarity within the SACNI.

4.4.6. The SACNI will be an executive with legislative capacities. It will have exclusive powers to make laws (by unanimous consent) with respect to

- matters relating to any department, authority or agency which is under its responsibility,

- civil defence and security,

- citizenship, nationality and immigration (subject to the laws of the European Community, and the Northern Ireland Bill of Rights and Fundamental Freedoms).

---

to reform the second chambers presently being advanced in both countries. In the absence of reform of the House of Lords and the Irish Senate we believe that the prime ministers of both states should be constitutionally obliged to appoint an appropriate and politically proportionate number of Northern Irish members to their respective second chambers - in the case of the Republic of Ireland this change could be exercised under Article 19 of *Bunreacht na hÉireann.*

A particular difficulty arises from the fact that a British minister from the House of Commons cannot be held to account by a committee of the House of Lords. On our proposals the nominated members of the SACNI will be accountable to the first chambers in Westminster and the Oireachtas, and their deputies (drawn from the House of Lords in the British case) will also appear before committees of the second chambers, which will include representatives from Northern Ireland.

* Many continental European governments and the European Council of Ministers operate successfully without the straightjacket of the Westminster model of collective responsibility.

The SACNI will have three main powers and functions:

- executive responsibility for matters which are not delegated to other authorities;

- executive responsibility for making ministerial, political and judicial appointments (including ministers, justices of the Supreme Court, the Attorney General,* and the Directorate of Public Prosecutions**);

- legislative capacities and rights of veto.

4.4.7. The SACNI will have ultimate responsibility for the defence and security of Northern Ireland. Under the terms of the Treaty establishing the Constitution of Northern Ireland the SACNI will be able to call in aid the armed forces of Great Britain and the Republic of Ireland. If these terms are activated the relevant forces will be subject to the supervision of the relevant appointed member of the SACNI. Unless there is complete consensus amongst the members of the SACNI on alternative arrangements we propose that the final authority for the police forces of Northern Ireland shall rest with the appointed members of the SACNI who will alternate this responsibility annually. They shall be responsible for determining any new structures for policing in the region. They may make arrangements for consulting other members of the SACNI on matters of security, and eventually, a security committee of the APNI.

4.4.8. The SACNI will appoint ministers to run government departments in Northern Ireland. The SACNI and the ministers can constitute an Executive Council, with the chair rotating between the members of the SACNI on a six-monthly basis.

---

* Given that the SACNI will require a law officer who has the confidence of the British and Irish governments we believe that the Attorney General should be appointed (and dismissed) by majority vote of the SACNI, providing that majority includes both the British and Irish nominees on the SACNI. The Attorney General shall not be a member of the SACNI or the APNI.

** We propose a Directorate rather than a Director of Public Prosecutions: a five person directorate appointed by the SACNI, each member of the SACNI appointing one director. In the event of the death or resignation of one director the entire directorate shall be re-appointed with each member of the SACNI appointing one director.

A MODEL OF SHARED AUTHORITY 31

- The ministers will be responsible for drafting legislation in consultation with the SACNI.
- They will be subject to interpellation but not dismissable by the Assembly. *
- They will, of course, be subject to legal accountability.
- Only persons willing to operate the Constitution of Northern Ireland will be eligible to be ministerial nominees.
- There shall be ministers of finance and justice.
- All ministers will follow a code of conduct laid before the APNI by the SACNI. A committee of the APNI may investigate any alleged breach of the code of conduct by ministers.

4.4.9. There are several ways in which ministers might be appointed by the SACNI. The simplest mechanism, which we favour, is for each member of the SACNI to be free to nominate (or dismiss) either one, two or three ministers (resulting in a total of five, ten or fifteen ministers). On this model we believe that the SACNI should be free to determine whether there should be five, ten or fifteen ministerial portfolios.

The allocation of ministerial nominees to specific portfolios could take place as a result of negotiations between SACNI members which required unanimity;
or by rank-ordering the right of nomination (so that the elected member with the highest level of voting support makes the first allocation, the elected member with the second highest level of voting support making the second allocation, the third elected member making the third allocation, the fourth allocation being made by either the British or Irish nominee (alternating their right to allocate persons to portfolios); and so on;
or by requiring allocations to specific portfolios to be made on the basis of a simple majority within the SACNI;

---

*   However, should the SACNI wish to change the government of Northern Ireland from a separation-of-powers regime to a more strictly parliamentary system we believe that provision should be made to enable ministers to be chosen from a panel elected by the Assembly of the Peoples of Northern Ireland, according to the Sainte-Laguë method as opposed to the d'Hondt method (to ensure that each political party obtains a proportional share of ministerial nominees - see Appendix B). However, the change from a separation-of-powers to a parliamentary regime should require the unanimous consent of the SACNI.

or by requiring allocations to be approved by both the British and Irish nominees as well as a majority on the SACNI; *or* by requiring preferential voting within the SACNI on nominees proposed for specific portfolios.*

4.4.10. Bills may be proposed to the SACNI on the initiative of a member of the SACNI or by ministers.

(a) If such bills receive the unanimous consent of the SACNI they are passed for scrutiny within a specified time-frame by the relevant committee of the APNI, which may propose amendments. The SACNI decides whether to accept these amendments by majority rule, providing the Speaker and Deputy Speaker have ruled that they are not wrecking amendments. The bills, as amended or not, then become law, subject only to receipt of the signature of the Monarch and the President.

(b) If such bills receive majority support in the SACNI they are considered by the next two meetings of the SACNI. Should they still have majority support within the SACNI they are then passed for scrutiny within a specified time-frame by the relevant committee of the APNI, which may propose amendments, and may propose according to a qualified majority rule (two thirds) that a vote on the bills be taken on the floor of the house. If the amendments receive the support of two thirds of the relevant committee the SACNI must accept them or drop the proposals. If the vote on the floor of the house is against the bills they are dropped. If the amendments receive majority support within the APNI committee the SACNI decides whether to accept these amendments by majority vote, providing the Speaker and Deputy Speaker have ruled that they are not wrecking amendments.

(c) If bills proposed by the SACNI are deemed fundamentally to affect national or religious rights and freedoms by either the Speaker or Deputy Speaker then they *may* require that the SACNI propose such bills only by unanimous consent. ** If the majority on the SACNI disagree with the Speaker or Deputy Speaker's

---

*   We have put forward various possible proposals to stimulate constructive thinking on possible constitutional designs for Northern Ireland.
**   The permissive formulation 'may' is intended to leave it to the judgement of the Speakers as to whether a bill intentionally and significantly affects national or religious rights and freedoms.

ruling on such bills they may ask the Supreme Court to rule on such bills.

The Assembly of the Peoples of Northern Ireland (APNI)

4.5. The Assembly of the Peoples of Northern Ireland shall be elected by proportional representation every four years (see Figure 4.2). It shall be first elected in the year after the establishment of the SACNI.

    4.5.1. The Assembly shall elect a Speaker and Deputy Speaker by means of a secret vote, in which each assembly member has one vote and the two highest placed candidates are elected. The Speaker and Deputy Speaker shall have equal standing in determining whether bills fundamentally threaten national or religious rights and freedoms, whether amendments proposed by committees are wrecking amendments, and in determining which committees shall scrutinise which bills.*

    4.5.2. The Assembly shall compose itself into committees which shall scrutinise the ministries established by the SACNI and a judicial committee. Chairships and representation on committees shall be determined by the Sainte-Laguë or the d'Hondt rule.**

---

* On present alignments these arrangements should ensure one speaker with the confidence of unionists and one speaker with the confidence of nationalists. (It may be considered preferable to require that a unionist speaker and nationalist speaker are always elected, but we do not wish to build in separate 'communal' constituencies into the constitution.) Where the Speaker and Deputy Speaker disagree on whether bills fundamentally threaten national or religious rights and freedoms, or on whether amendments are wrecking amendments, their disagreements may be sent for consideration to the Supreme Court by one or both of them. This mechanism will provide an incentive for the Speaker and Deputy Speaker to co-operate to preserve their autonomy and that of the Assembly, compared with the executive and the judiciary.
** Under the d'Hondt rule the number of committee chairs each party holds in the assembly is determined by successively dividing their percentage of seats in the assembly by 1, 2, 3, 4 ... (Appendix B). Instead of the d'Hondt rule (which usually helps large parties) some version of the Sainte-Laguë rule might be used instead (which usually ensures better proportionality, especially for medium sized and smaller parties). Under the Sainte-Laguë rule the number of committee chairs each party holds in the assembly is determined by successively

A MODEL OF SHARED AUTHORITY

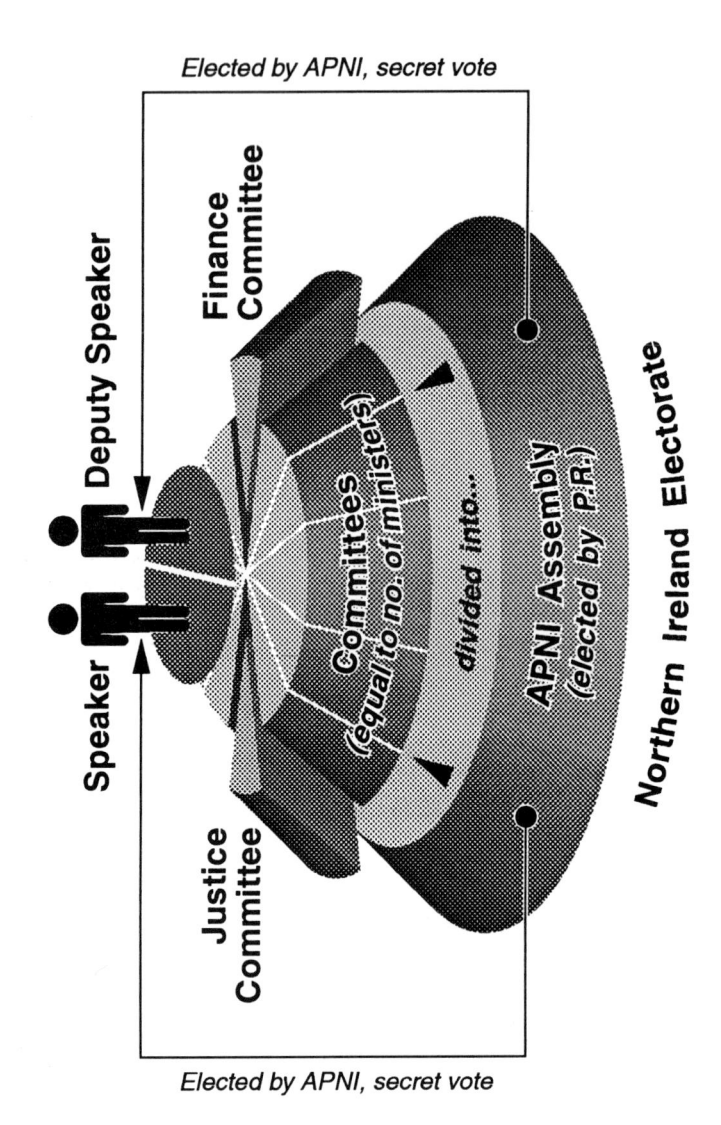

Elected by APNI, secret vote

Elected by APNI, secret vote

Figure 4.2

---

dividing the number of seats each party holds in the assembly by 1, 3, 5 (Appendix B contains an extended discussion).

A MODEL OF SHARED AUTHORITY 35

These committees shall be responsible for scrutinising the conduct of ministerial departments and considering bills proposed by the SACNI. The Speaker and Deputy Speaker shall decide which committee has jurisdiction over a bill proposed by the SACNI. The committees shall have the power to summon witnesses and to examine government documents - saving only those protected by security requirements which shall be examinable by the judicial committee of the APNI. The committees shall also have the powers specified in paragraph 4.4.10.

4.5.3. The APNI shall have exclusive powers to make laws with respect to locating the seat or seats of government of Northern Ireland. Thus the APNI shall be free to determine the geographical location of the Supreme Court, the SACNI and the APNI.

4.6. Bills may be proposed by any committee of the Assembly if they obtain the support of two thirds of the members of the committee. They are then put to a vote on the floor of the assembly. If they are passed there by a similar majority they become law unless they are vetoed by the SACNI, which may veto such bills on a majority vote of the SACNI. Should any such bill not be vetoed by the SACNI any dissatisfied member of the SACNI is entitled to challenge the constitutionality of any such law before the Supreme Court. The making of laws under our proposed model of shared authority is summarised in Figure 4.3.

4.7. Provision shall be made for ministers to be interpellated by committees, to deal with constituency representations, and to answer debates on the conduct of the SACNI. Members of the SACNI may be invited to address the APNI and vice versa.

4.8. Sessions of the APNI shall be opened by the Monarch and the President or their representatives.

4.9. The Finance Committee of the APNI shall not have the power to propose financial bills - although it shall be entitled to scrutinise such bills, propose amendments in the normal manner (except for financial bills supporting security expenditures), and to interpellate the relevant minister.

4.10. Each committee of the APNI shall be able to scrutinise ministerial appointments to public bodies within their jurisdiction.

36 A MODEL OF SHARED AUTHORITY

HEAD OF STATE

Monarch of United Kingdom *and* President of Ireland

Bills for signature by

SACNI

Accepted by SACNI with majority consent for non-wrecking amendments

Bill subject to SACNI simple majority veto

Bill Proposal by SACNI passed to Speakers

SACNI must accept non-wrecking amendments or drop bill

Unanimous Consent (including bills on national, & religious freedoms)

Majority Consent 3 meetings of SACNI (other bills)

Speakers

Proposed amendments by relevant committee (majority agreement)

Proposed amendments passed with 2/3 majority

Committees

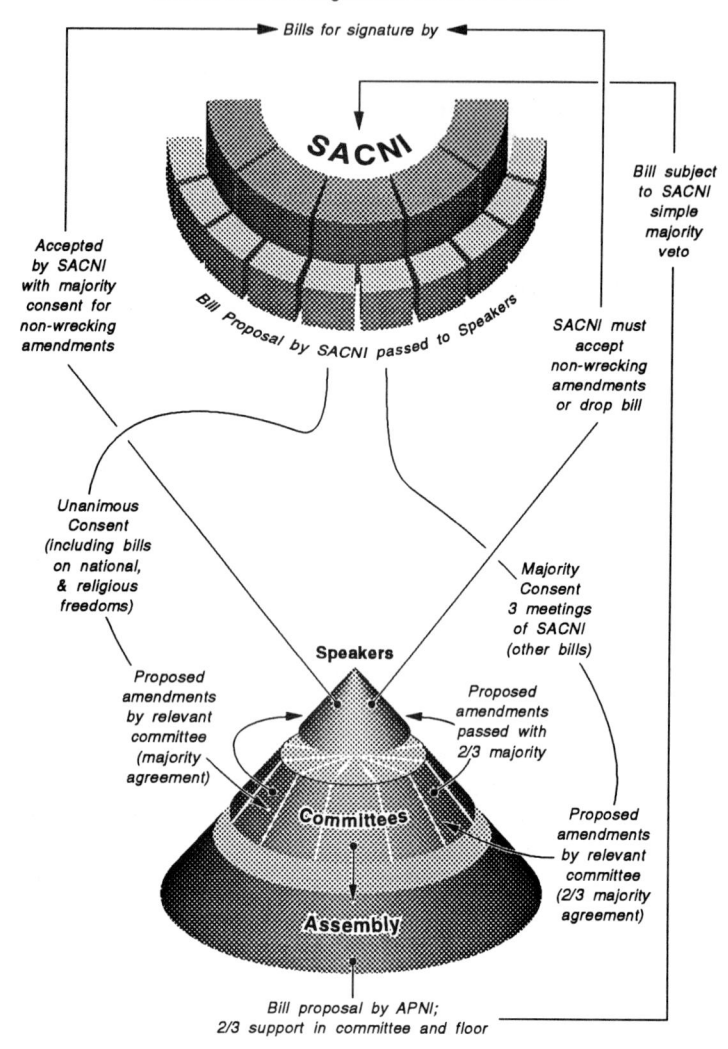

Proposed amendments by relevant committee (2/3 majority agreement)

Assembly

Bill proposal by APNI; 2/3 support in committee and floor

Figure 4.3

A MODEL OF SHARED AUTHORITY   37

4.11. Provided there is broad consensus within the APNI - an extraordinary majority of three quarters - the APNI may choose to permit the Speaker and Deputy Speaker to constitute such permanent or *ad hoc* committees as they see fit.

Supreme Court and the Judicial System

4.12. Under shared authority Northern Ireland will necessarily acquire an autonomous legal personality: neither the legal systems of the United Kingdom nor of the Republic of Ireland could provide the supreme court without introducing imbalance into any model of shared authority. Northern Ireland's Constitution will therefore be subject to the jurisdiction of Northern Ireland's Supreme Court - although we envisage its decisions, where appropriate, being made subject to appeals to the European Court of Human Rights and the European Court of Justice. We propose the following arrangements for the composition of the Supreme Court.

- There shall be five justices on the Supreme Court. Each member of the first SACNI shall have the right to nominate one justice of the first Supreme Court, and these nominees shall then be subject to collective ratification by the judicial committee of the APNI when that body is elected. This committee shall be able to veto the appointment of the SACNI's nominees once only; the second set of nominees shall be automatically appointed.

- The Chief Justice shall be elected by his or her peers, and hold office for five years. He or she may be re-elected.

- If justices of the Supreme Court retire or die during the period of office of the first SACNI they shall be replaced by the nominee of the SACNI member who proposed the justice who has died or retired. His or her appointment will be scrutinised by the judicial committee of the APNI.

- Thereafter new members of the Supreme Court shall be nominated with the consent of a majority of the SACNI - including the consent of the British and Irish nominees - and shall be subject to the ratification of the judicial committee of the APNI. The latter may reject a nominee solely on the grounds of legal incompetence or of demonstrably inappropriate character. A list of suitably qualified candidates shall be maintained by a Judicial Services Commission for Northern Ireland, and shall be broader than the pool from which judges are presently drawn.

- Provision shall be made for alternative arrangements for the appointment of justices to be agreed by the unanimous consent of the SACNI and the judicial committee of the APNI.

- Figure 4.4. illustrates the nature of the proposed Supreme Court.

4.13. Other judges in Northern Ireland will be appointed according to a professional public appointment system. Posts will be advertised and appointments will be made by the Judicial Services Commission for Northern Ireland which will consist of judicial, legal and lay members. The Commission will be required to ensure a balanced representation of both communities. As with membership of the Supreme Court, the pool from which judges will be drawn will be broader than at present. The entire workings of the judicial system will be open to the scrutiny of the judicial committee of the APNI. Appropriate methods will need to be devised for proceeding with the impeachment of a corrupt or incompetent judge.

4.14. The laws of Northern Ireland shall be those presently in force, save as modified by the international treaty establishing the Constitution of Northern Ireland, the Bill of Rights and other provisions protecting fundamental rights and freedoms. * We believe it would be appropriate to accompany these changes with a new criminal justice system - in which there would be three judge courts for 'certified-in' scheduled offences. The SACNI shall be the relevant governmental authority responsible before the European Court of Justice for the execution of European Community law.

Bill of Rights and Protection of Fundamental Freedoms

4.15. The Treaty establishing shared authority must protect the civil, individual and cultural rights of all citizens of Northern Ireland. The Treaty should therefore incorporate a Bill of Rights, in the form of the European Convention on Human Rights, into the domestic law of Northern Ireland.** This Bill of Rights, like other rights provisions, will be subject to interpretation by the Supreme Court.

---

* We think it would be advisable for the British government to clarify and strengthen the *Fair Employment Act* (1989) before passage of the Treaty creating shared authority.

** We are aware of the debates on the inadequacies of the European Convention but it does provide minimum standards common to Britain

A MODEL OF SHARED AUTHORITY 39

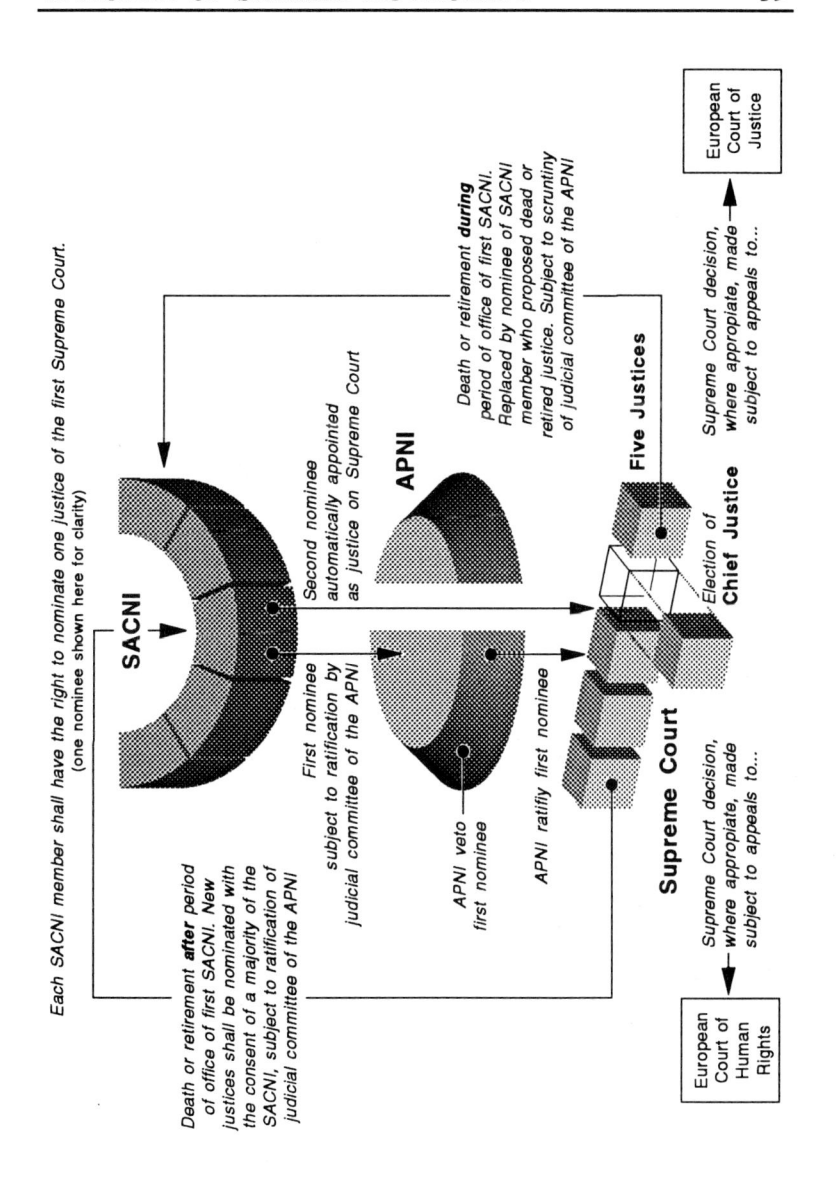

Figure 4.4

and Ireland and is understood by the courts in legal jurisdictions in these islands.

4.16. The incorporation of the Bill of Rights and the Constitution should be qualified by three clauses to protect equality rights, and by provisions to protect collective cultural rights. The 'equality rights' might be stated as follows:

4.16. 1. Every individual is equal before and under the law and has the right to the equal protection and benefit of the law without direct or indirect discrimination, and, in particular, without direct or indirect discrimination based on religion, political opinion, race, national or ethnic origin, colour, sex, sexual orientation, age or mental or physical disability.

4.16.2.
(a) The SACNI shall ensure that material inequalities between Roman Catholics and Protestants shall be progressively reduced, and shall bring forward measures and policies which in the judgement of the SACNI will do so.
(b) Clause 4.16.1. shall not preclude any law, public policy programme or activity, like the *Fair Employment Act* (1989), that has as its object the amelioration of conditions of disadvantaged individuals or groups, specifically those that are disadvantaged because of their religion, race, national or ethnic origin, colour, sex, sexual orientation, age, or (mental or physical) disability. No other article of the Constitution may be invoked to limit this provision.

4.16.3. Nothing in the Bill of Rights abrogates or derogates from any rights or privileges guaranteed by or under the Constitution of Northern Ireland in respect of denominational, separate or dissentient schools.*

4.17. The operation of the Bill of the Rights and the Constitution should also be qualified by provisions protecting collective cultural rights - including rights of cultural expression, the use of the English and Irish languages, and religious and non-religious education. These rights should include

---

* These proposed provisions are modelled on clauses 15 and 29 of the Canadian *Charter of Rights and Freedoms* (Ottawa, 1982) which ensures that neither the freedom of conscience and religion clauses nor the equality rights clauses can be interpreted so as to strike down existing rights respecting the establishment and state-financing of schools operated on a religious basis, with students and teachers selected according to their adherence to a particular religious faith.

4.17.1. Either a general provision recognising the equal validity of the unionist and nationalist traditions and cultures*, or the insertion of specific enactments of constitutional provisions requiring appropriate public bodies - such as the composers of publicly examinable educational curricula and public broadcasting authorities - to give equal consideration and fair treatment to the two major traditions.

4.17.2. The formal recognition of the right of all parents to have their children educated in schools of a particular character - e.g. Roman Catholic, Protestant (of whatever denomination), Jewish, integrated, Irish-medium, and non-religious - with equivalent public funding where the numbers involved justified such expenditure, providing that such schools follow the minimal requirements of the publicly examinable curriculum.

4.17.3. The formal requirement that relevant public bodies be competent to communicate with citizens in the Irish language, with equivalent public funding for such personnel as may be required where the numbers involved justified such expenditure. **

External Relations

4.18. We have already stated that it follows logically from the structures of co-sovereignty that Northern Ireland must become an autonomous legal jurisdiction, autonomous from both Britain and the Republic of Ireland. For this reason we have proposed an autonomous Supreme Court, subject only to appeals to European Courts. Given this recognition of Northern Ireland's separate legal personality we believe it is consistent with our model of shared authority for Northern Ireland to be free to develop autonomous, but not independent, external relations, especially for the purposes of negotiating Northern Ireland's interests in the European Community.

4.18.1. Initially we propose that the British and Irish nominees on the SACNI represent Northern Ireland's external interests in the

---

* Care would have to be taken to ensure that those features of the republican and loyalist traditions which are incitements to hatred do not receive constitutional protection.
** These proposed provisions are based on the work of the Standing Advisory Commission on Human Rights *Religious and Political Discrimination and Equality of Opportunity in Northern Ireland: Second Report* (London, HMSO, 1990).

respective cabinet/government, and alternate annually in representing - or delegating to an appropriate colleague - Northern Ireland's interests in the European Council of Ministers. Provided shared authority proved durable we believe it would then be possible for British and Irish ministers to negotiate a special form of representation for Northern Ireland at European Community level - either through the elected members of the SACNI being consulted by the Council of Ministers and the Commission, or Northern Ireland's Members of the European Parliament being specially consulted by the Council of Ministers and the Commission.

4.18.2. It would also be appropriate for Northern Ireland to be autonomously represented by elected local government representatives in the European Committee of the Regions.

4.18.3. The SACNI must be free to negotiate international agreements affecting citizens, companies and public bodies in Northern Ireland - subject to the explicit approval of both the British and Irish nominees on the SACNI.

4.18.4. Citizens and residents of Northern Ireland travelling or resident outside these islands should be entitled to seek access to ambassadorial and conciliar services of either the British or Irish governments.

4.18.5. Northern Ireland shall become an autonomous member of the British Commonwealth of Nations - which it may leave only after a referendum conducted under the rules governing changes to the constitution of Northern Ireland.

4.18.6. Northern Ireland shall be militarily protected by both the United Kingdom government and the government of the Republic of Ireland. It shall be an implied party to any new defensive or military alliance entered into by the United Kingdom government and the government of the Republic of Ireland.

Durability and the Constitutional Status of Northern Ireland

4.19. Durability is an essential ingredient in the success of any model of shared authority. We do not see our model of shared authority as a short-term or transitional proposal. There are many ways to ensure the durability of our model, and we outline our preferred methods below. Our proposals would entrench Northern Ireland's dual status in the

A MODEL OF SHARED AUTHORITY 43

public law of the United Kingdom, the Constitution of Ireland, and the Constitution of Northern Ireland. We have spelled out this status above (in paragraph 4.3.), and believe it should form the first article of the Constitution of Northern Ireland, and should be incorporated into British public law and Irish constitutional law (see paragraph 4.19.2). The second way of ensuring the durability of shared authority is to make it difficult to change the status of Northern Ireland. To this end we put forward in paragraph 4.20 a proposal for the constitutional entrenchment of our suggested model.

4.19.1. We believe that an entrenchment clause, like that outlined in paragraph 4.20, is essential to reassure unionists that shared authority is not a transitional mechanism for coercing them into a territorially unified Ireland; to reassure northern nationalists that shared authority is not a transitional mechanism for coercing them into an independent Northern Ireland; and to make the Constitution compatible with necessary revisions of the Irish Constitution and British public law.

4.19.2. We believe that any constitutional entrenchment clauses should define the status of Northern Ireland as specified in 4.3. above. Moreover, this dual constitutional status of Northern Ireland should be mutually recognised in British public law and the Irish Constitution. In the British version of the Treaty establishing shared authority it should state as follows:

'(i) The national territory of the United Kingdom, as modified by the following clause, includes Northern Ireland, its islands and territorial seas.

(ii) Northern Ireland is the national territory of both the British and Irish nations and states, and shall remain so until such time as the peoples of Northern Ireland decide otherwise according to the provisions of the Constitution of Northern Ireland. No provision of British constitutional or public law invalidates laws enacted, acts done or measures adopted by the state necessitated by the Treaty on shared authority in regard to Northern Ireland entered into by the Government of the United Kingdom.'

Consistent with the above we believe that the following amendments should be made to Articles 2 and 3 of the Constitution of Ireland. Article 2 should read

'The national territory of Ireland, as modified by Article 3, consists of the whole island of Ireland, its islands and its territorial seas.'

Article 3 should be amended to read as follows:

'3 (a) Northern Ireland is the national territory of both the Irish and British nations and states, and shall remain so until such time as the peoples of Northern Ireland decide otherwise according to the provisions of the Constitution of Northern Ireland.
3 (b) No provision of this Constitution invalidates laws enacted, acts done or measures adopted by the state necessitated by the Treaty on shared authority in regard to Northern Ireland entered into by the Irish Government and People'.*

Mechanism for Changing the Constitutional Status of Northern Ireland

4.20. To ensure the durability of shared authority we believe the status of Northern Ireland should be additionally qualified by a clause, embedded in the international Treaty and the Constitution of Northern Ireland, along the following lines

'The constitutional status of Northern Ireland as an autonomous political region which is part of the national territory of both the Republic of Ireland and the United Kingdom may be changed only through a referendum in which the consent of three quarters of the turnout of the electorally registered citizens of Northern Ireland has been obtained'. **

We further suggest that

---

* It is entirely for the Irish people to amend their Constitution through a popular referendum. However, we believe that without changes to Articles 2 and 3 along the lines proposed above the constitutional model proposed here could not work effectively.
** An alternative weighted majority might insist on a less demanding threshold of two-thirds support for change. However, this threshold might precipitate an immediate crisis for our model of shared authority because at present all unionist parties - defining the Alliance Party, the Conservatives and Democratic Left as small 'u' unionists - attract just less than two thirds of the electorate, while all northern nationalist parties attract just over one third of the electorate.

- it should not be possible to hold such a referendum until five years have elapsed since the election of the first SACNI, and only on every tenth year thereafter;
- such a referendum may only be held after a petition has been approved by two thirds of the APNI and a majority of the members of the SACNI, and after the Supreme Court has ruled that the question to be posed in the referendum is unambiguous;
- if the petition for a referendum proposes that Northern Ireland become wholly part of the Republic of Ireland or wholly part of the United Kingdom the referendum should not take place before the executive and legislature of the affected state consent to the possible incorporation of Northern Ireland into their exclusive jurisdiction.

The merits of this proposal are that it is balanced and fair. It protects equally the current minority and a possible future minority from being exclusively incorporated into one state's jurisdiction against its will. It is constitutionally neutral on the future of Northern Ireland - permitting Irish unification, re-establishment of the unqualified Union, independence, and other possible variations on Northern Ireland's constitutional status. It has a very good feature for unionists, it protects them better than they are at protected at present; and it has a very good feature for northern nationalists, because it does the same. Its weakness may be considered to be that Northern Ireland's constitutional status might be considered too inflexible, but we are persuaded that that is its key virtue. It will provide a key element of certainty. Any weaker form of entrenchment would be seen as weighted in the interest of northern nationalists (especially in the light of present demographic trends and beliefs) and therefore would not provide the stability required to make shared authority work.

4.21 It is of course possible to disagree with our proposal on how to entrench the durability of shared authority. Some, especially northern nationalists, might argue that a lower threshold of change should be required to change the status of Northern Ireland. They might argue that its constitutional status should be changed only through a referendum, held in say twenty years, in which the consent of a majority of the electorally registered citizens of Northern Ireland was obtained. We have also heard arguments that such a referendum should not propose independence for Northern Ireland. The rationale for this thinking is that it would permit a simple majority to change the status of Northern Ireland - hopefully after a period of successful co-operative government. It is not, however, neutral on the future direction of constitutional change, because it rules out independence - as did the drafters of the Anglo-Irish Agreement. We have heard people argue that it would be fair to keep the existing simple majority provisions for changing the status of Northern Ireland because it would not 'change the goal-posts' for Irish unification - as envisaged under the Anglo-Irish Agreement. However, we strongly disagree with such arguments. The fundamental case for shared authority rests on its fairness (see Chapter 5). Any proposal for shared authority which does not equally protect each community would be unfair and unworkable. Majoritarian constitutional designs have failed Northern Ireland in the past, and majoritarian ideas for establishing its status have not resolved conflict over its status in the past, so there are no grounds for believing that resolving Northern Ireland's constitutional status by a simple majoritarian mechanism is a good idea.* Our proposals are therefore consistent with the principles of constitutional design which we outlined and defended in Chapter 3.

Provisions for Changing the Constitution other than Northern Ireland's Constitutional Status

4.22. We believe that proposed constitutional changes for Northern Ireland - other than those which would affect its dual status as part of the British and Irish nations - should require a high threshold of agreement, but not as high as that required for changing the constitutional status of Northern Ireland: a two thirds majority of the turnout of validly registered citizens in a referendum (which can be initiated either by a petition attracting 200,000 signatures or by a majority in the APNI and the SACNI).

Administration and Local Government

4.23. Under our model of shared authority the Northern Ireland Office would be replaced by a Secretariat which served the SACNI. The Secretariat could include persons seconded from the British and Irish civil services but we envisage a civil service drawn primarily from the citizens of Northern Ireland. The civil service will be recruited so that it is socially representative of the communities of Northern Ireland, and respect the principles of proportionality inherent in this constitutional design.

4.24. Local government, by definition, is something which should be structured and determined in ways agreed by the new political authorities in Northern Ireland. It would therefore be inappropriate for us to pre-empt the design of the boundaries, institutions and functions

---

* Further reasons for our mode of retrenchment are advanced in Chapters 5 and 6.

A MODEL OF SHARED AUTHORITY 47

of local government. For the time being we envisage that the present system would remain, but that the SACNI with the approval of the APNI should have the right to delegate functions to local governments, provided they are consistent with Article 1 of the Constitution of Northern Ireland as proposed in paragraph 4.3. above. We hope that the SACNI and the APNI would see the value in enhancing the degree of responsibility and accountability of local governments. However, that is a matter for the future political authorities of Northern Ireland. Constitutional provisions will need to be made to ensure that local government boundaries and electoral districts do not violate anti-discrimination clauses in the Constitution, and to establish independent boundary commissions.

State of Emergency

4.25. Where in the opinion of both the nominated members of the SACNI, in Northern Ireland or any part of Northern Ireland, a grave threat to public security or public order has arisen, or is likely to arise, or a grave civil emergency has arisen, or is likely to arise, they may by executive decree, make provision, to the extent strictly required by the exigencies of the situation and reasonably justified in a democratic society, suspending, in whole or in part, absolutely or subject to conditions, any of the provisions of the Constitution. This decree must be ratified by the British cabinet and the Irish government, and must be renewed at six-monthly intervals after debates in the respective parliaments of the co-sovereign powers and the APNI (if sitting). This power shall not be used

- to change the constitutional status of Northern Ireland;

- to suspend a citizen's right to life (except in respect of deaths resulting from lawful acts of war), or the rights to be protected from torture, inhuman or degrading treatment, slavery, or discrimination, or the right to freedom of thought and worship;

- to create retrospective offences.

In such an emergency disagreements between the British and Irish nominees on the SACNI may be resolved through binding arbitration by a committee of three EC foreign ministers (consisting of those who presently (a) hold the EC presidency, (b) have just held the EC presidency, and (c) will next hold the EC presidency *) **.

Implementation

4.26. How could our model of shared authority be implemented ? That is partly a matter for debate, reflection, and public persuasion - to which this book is offered as a contribution. It is essential to the success of a model of shared authority that it be broadly attractive to an Irish government and its people, who will need to support the idea in a constitutional referendum. We can see no reason, in principle, why it should not be attractive to the people of the Republic of Ireland. In the Republic there is widespread willingness to accept a 'British dimension' in any future settlement of Northern Ireland. In the JRRT/Gallup polls conducted in 1991 40 per cent of the Republic's citizens envisage a minor role for the British government in the future of Northern Ireland, and 28 per cent a major role - compared with just 24 per cent of nationalists who see no function for the British to perform. There is naturally even stronger enthusiasm for an Irish dimension, with 57 per cent supporting a major role for their government and 31 per cent a minor role.

4.27. It is equally essential to the success of a model of shared authority that it be broadly attractive to a British government and its people, who will also need to support the idea. From the same polls the evidence is that citizens of Great Britain are very willing to give the Irish government a major role in any new settlement (49 per cent), with only 11 per cent expressing the wish to exclude the Irish government completely. [12] For these reasons we believe that the British and Irish governments could carry their electorates with them in agreeing to construct and implement a model of shared authority for Northern Ireland.

---

*   If one of these ministers is a British or Irish minister then the foreign minister next in succession shall be asked to sit on this committee.
**   The state of emergency will have to be notified to the Council of Europe. A declaration of a state of emergency could be made conditional upon approval from the Council of Europe. However, the only Council of Europe institution presently capable of giving an immediate response is the Council of Ministers which is unlikely to refuse such a request. If this process was followed then any subsequent challenge to the legality of the emergency would become much more difficult.

A MODEL OF SHARED AUTHORITY

4.27. Naturally it will be initially more difficult to persuade all people in Northern Ireland of the merits of shared authority. The arguments which follow are designed to persuade them of its merits. We think that it would be appropriate for the British and Irish governments to table proposals along these lines for discussion at any inter-party and inter-governmental talks. Should they play a role in allowing the parties to reach an agreement we will be more than satisfied. However, should such talks fail to bear fruit we believe it would be appropriate for the British and Irish governments to recognise that to work successfully shared authority need not initially have widespread consent amongst the peoples of Northern Ireland. No other proposals presently enjoy widespread support across both communities. In the event of deadlocked negotiations between the parties in Northern Ireland the two governments should follow and improve on the path they embraced when they signed the Anglo-Irish Agreement, and develop an agreement between the two governments, along the lines indicated here, which can be subsequently worked with by politicians and their communities in Northern Ireland because it will be in their interests to make it work. However, we also believe that if people can be persuaded of our arguments it is more likely that a voluntarily agreed system of shared authority will become more widely recognised as the fair and rational way to resolve the existing crisis.

CHAPTER 5   THE POSITIVE CASE

5.1. The case for sharing authority, responsibility and power, shared authority for short, could be made negatively, simply by arguing that it is the least bad proposal for the future of Northern Ireland. And indeed shared authority, as we envisage it, has a number of major advantages which other options cannot offer, and we show why that is so in some detail below. [13] However, the positive advantages of sharing authority, responsibility and power are worth stating first in their own right, as they offer a simultaneously imaginative and realistic way of regulating a severe national and ethnic conflict with religious dimensions. Shared authority is not merely the most feasible of the desirable solutions it is also the most desirable of the feasible solutions. Naturally shared authority is not a panacea, and its development and implementation will involve a number of problems which we address below.

5.2. The benefits of the system of shared authority which we elaborate below are divisible into four inter-related dimensions.

- *Fairness.* Sharing authority, responsibility and power will guarantee national and cultural equality to both communities within Northern Ireland, and sovereign equality to their respective states, the United Kingdom and the Republic of Ireland.

- *Accountable and representative democratic government.* Sharing authority, responsibility and power are compatible with liberal democratic norms of participation and accountability, and our system proposed below has built-in 'democratic multipliers' to encourage political accommodation between the two communities in Northern Ireland. It ensures that each community can have proportional representation in political institutions, self-government on cultural matters, and constitutional safeguards to protect their identities and interests. [14]

- *Security.* Sharing authority, responsibility and power will establish a security-system which will diminish the capacities of paramilitaries and the rationale for paramilitary violence, and its prospects of damaging democratic political institutions. Shared authority will also facilitate the establishment of widely legitimate legal and policing institutions.

- *Economic feasibility.* Sharing authority, responsibility and power is not only compatible with principles of fiscal equity and accountability, but, as we shall show below, consistent with the economic interests of all the parties concerned.

Fairness

5.3. If a conflict between two parties is 'zero-sum' then only one side can win, or, alternatively, the two sides can take it in turns to win or lose. The worst kind of conflict is called 'negative sum' because all participants end up worse off because of their disagreements. Few would quarrel with the idea that Northern Ireland varies between being a zero-sum and a negative sum conflict. When confronted with such situations the best option is to transform the 'rules of the game' so that the agents can co-operate to their mutual advantage, so that both gain from changing their behaviour. That is precisely the nature of the thinking behind our proposals for shared authority.

5.4. The key 'rule of the game' which keeps Northern Ireland locked in conflict is 'the false assumption that the "cliffs of sovereignty go sheer into the sea", and that a choice has to be made between unalloyed British rule from London or Irish rule from Dublin.' [15] The rule of indivisible sovereignty is all the more difficult to change because so many people believe that sovereignty has an 'all or nothing' character, an idea deeply embedded in British and Irish political culture. This idea is also connected to the majoritarian tradition of politics in Great Britain, Northern Ireland and the Republic (at least until 1989) in which government like sovereignty has been seen as a question of 'winner takes all'.

5.5. The fairness of sharing sovereignty has appealed to many who have addressed the need to have constructive proposals for the government of Northern Ireland. A range of independent academics and thinkers in Britain and Ireland have advocated some variation on shared authority or condominial structures for Northern Ireland, and many continue to do so. In both parts of Ireland arguments in favour of sharing sovereignty have been articulated by F.W. Boal and J.N.H. Douglas (political geographers based in Belfast), Basil Chubb (a political scientist, based in Trinity College, Dublin), Bernard Cullen (a political philosopher from a unionist background), Desmond Fennell (a cultural critic and Irish nationalist), Richard Kearney (a philosopher), and Frank Wright (a British-born political scientist). [16] In Britain arguments against exclusive British sovereignty over Northern Ireland have been made by Bernard Crick (a political philosopher), by Martin

Dent (a political scientist), T.J. Pickvance (an academic at Birmingham University), and by the persons who sat on the independent Kilbrandon inquiry. [17] The Opsahl Report, published in 1993, which gathered together submissions and ideas from people within and outside of Northern Ireland received 33 submissions which suggested 'various forms of administering Northern Ireland with an input from both the British and Irish governments (the third most popular category of suggested political structures)'. [18]

5.6. The concluding paragraph of the New Ireland Forum *Report* signed by all the major constitutional nationalist parties in Ireland (Fianna Fáil, Fine Gael, the Irish Labour Party and the Social Democratic and Labour Party of Northern Ireland) pointed out that
> 'Under joint authority the two traditions in Northern Ireland would find themselves on a basis of equality and both would be able to find an expression of their identity in the new institutions. There would be no diminution of the Britishness of the unionist population. Their identity, ethos and link with Britain would be assured by the authority and presence of the British Government in the joint authority arrangements. At the same time it would resolve one basic defect of (a) the failed 1920-25 attempt to settle the Irish question and (b) the present arrangements for the government of Northern Ireland - the failure to give satisfactory political, symbolic and administrative expression to Northern nationalists'. [19]

The key argument advanced at the New Ireland Forum was that both communities in Northern Ireland would gain from shared authority because their national identity, political security and civic equality would be mutually guaranteed. The citizens of the two communities would have guaranteed membership of their preferred state's institutions, and have access, on a voluntary basis, to the institutions of citizenship provided by the other state.

Fairness for Nationalists

5.7. It is perhaps easy to see why Irish nationalists, especially northern nationalists, might see fairness in some version of shared authority. For northern nationalists it would mark a significant improvement in the status quo. Their national identity would be institutionally expressed on an equal footing with that of unionists. Their status would be upgraded. Under shared authority the government of the Republic of Ireland, which northern nationalists have seen as their rightful ruler, prospective ruler, or as the guardian of their interests, would play an increased policy-formulation and policy-implementation role, a more significant one than it presently plays under the Anglo-Irish Agreement. Most northern nationalists would be well pleased by such a constitutional change: according to the JRRT/UMS poll conducted in the summer of 1991 95 per cent of Catholics in Northern Ireland would like to see the Irish government playing either a major or minor role in the government of Northern Ireland. [20]

5.8. Nationalist political parties throughout Ireland have also backed joint authority on regular occasions. In 1972 the SDLP proposed a condominial structure for Northern Ireland. Fianna Fáil, Fine Gael, the Irish Labour Party (ILP) and the SDLP, who between them consistently take over 90 per cent of the nationalist vote in Ireland as a whole, committed themselves to joint authority as their third most-preferred option for the future of Northern Ireland at the New Ireland Forum in 1984. In 1992 the SDLP proposed an executive version of joint authority in the inter-party talks organised by the two governments, involving commissioners from Britain, the Republic (and the European Community). Therefore there should be little difficulty in persuading constitutional Irish nationalists of the merits of a system of sharing authority, responsibility and power.

5.9. However, it must be squarely recognised that shared authority would not be regarded as fair by militant republicans who believe that the only just solution involves the complete termination of British sovereignty over any part of Ireland. They think that *any* British governmental role in Northern Ireland is illegitimate. They claim that the partition of Ireland in 1920 was unfair because it denied the Irish people 'as a whole' their right to self-determination: for them Northern Ireland is an artificial and unjustifiable entity. This viewpoint, although it is not entirely devoid of merit, is partial, and exposing its partiality confirms the fairness of the idea of shared authority.

5.10. The partition of Ireland in 1920 was indeed illegitimate because the Government of Ireland Act of 1920 was not supported by any Irish MPs [21], or by a referendum, and, more importantly, because the particular pattern of partition imposed was unfair. On any reasonable construal of the doctrine of self-determination far more people and territory should have been incorporated in the Irish Free State in the 1920s either in the Anglo-Irish Treaty or as an outcome of the Boundary Commission which it proposed. [22] However, that said, unless one dogmatically accepts the republican assumption that the entire island of Ireland was the only possible unit in which the political future of Ireland should have been decided, it must be concluded that militant republicans have an unanswerable case only against the pattern of partition rather than against partition itself.

5.11. Any liberal theory of self-determination, we believe, points *either* towards the merits of re-partitioning Ireland *or* towards sharing sovereignty over Northern Ireland. If we can show that is so, and also demonstrate that if confronted with the choice between shared authority and re-partition most republicans would favour shared authority, then we will have underlined the fairness of shared authority for nationalists.

5.12. The fairest way in which the most liberal principle of self-determination (including the right of secession) should be exercised is as follows:
any self-defined people in a given territory should have the right to secede from an existing state, provided (a) they express their consent to secession, and (b) give the same right to any people within a sub-unit of the area proposed for secession. *

---

*   Harry Beran 'A Liberal Theory of Secession' *Political Studies* (xxxii, 1984) and see also his book *The Consent Theory of Political Obligation* (London, 1987). Beran's theory of self-determination is hedged about by qualifications - relating to 'political and economic circumstances' - but its normative presumption in favour of the right to self-determination is clear and defensible. This theory which allows for 'self-determination within self-determination' is not, of course, recognised in current 'international law'. Indeed insofar as there is an international law of self-determination it allows self-determination only for existing majorities in existing states or for regions defined as colonies, i.e. self-determination only applies to states and colonial territories. We think that for obvious reasons the present international law of self-determination is morally and politically worthless, even if it continues to be defended by the General Secretary of the United Nations.

However, insofar as international law is considered valid and operational, it is most reasonably construed as offering support for the republican position because it is supposed to prohibit the partition of regions due for decolonisation - i.e. it prohibits what occurred in Ireland during 1920-21. It is for this reason, amongst others, that Northern Ireland is considered internationally illegitimate - see for example A. Guelke *Northern Ireland : The International Perspective* (Dublin: 1988)). Unionists would claim, in contrast, that neither Ireland nor Northern Ireland were colonies, that the Irish Free State recognised Northern Ireland in 1921 and 1925, and that therefore the international law of self-determination legitimises Northern Ireland's present status as part of the United Kingdom. Republicans would reply that these so-called 'recognitions' were coerced - the Treaty by threat

The intuitive fairness of this idea is obvious: the right of self-determination should apply to everybody, majorities as well as minorities. Its practical efficacy, of course, is more debatable, especially when there cannot easily be territorial contiguity and separateness for each successive seceding unit. However, this principle, formulated by political philosopher Harry Beran, does provide a liberal normative standard against which to assess claims for self-determination. The secession of the Irish Free State from the United Kingdom was fair by this criterion: in the 1918 Westminster elections 95 per cent of the electorate in what became the Irish Free State endorsed parties or candidates supporting republican independence or extensive autonomy for Ireland. The same principle can also be used to justify the argument that a very considerable proportion of the population of the north-east of Ireland had the right to opt-out of the secession of the rest of Ireland from the United Kingdom. However, this same principle cannot be used to justify the particular border given to Northern Ireland in 1920, which left a very significant minority, at least 30 per cent of its electorate, without the ability to exercise its right to self-determination.

5.13. This discursus into the political philosophy of self-determination might suggest both the historical and present merits of a better partition of Ireland. Such an argument could indeed be made, and has been made by a minority of intellectuals, but it is not one that we endorse, in part because of the moral and practical difficulties associated with re-partition (see Chapter 6. § 16-17). It is no part of our purpose to advocate re-partition. However, we do maintain, contrary to republicans, that a liberal theory of self-determination, to which republicans implicitly appeal in their arguments, does not suggest the justice of a united Ireland, but rather the justice of a re-partition now to make amends for the unjust partition of 1920. If so, what follows ? What is the force of this argument ? It follows, we believe, that if there are other compelling reasons for rejecting re-partition then any believer in a liberal theory of self-determination must advocate a form of government for Northern Ireland which enables both the present majority and the present minority in the region to exercise self-

---

of war, and the Boundary Commission by a biased review. These conflicting interpretations of international law show how unhelpful is its present reading of self determination and its lack of utility in resolving the problems of Northern Ireland.

We accept, however, that the international law of human rights can play an important and constructive role in the constitutional reconstruction of Northern Ireland.

determination to the greatest degree possible. That in turn means enabling both communities to belong to and be governed through their preferred nation-state. Shared authority is the only way of realising this objective.

5.14. The moral and political force of this argument against the militant republican position on self-determination is compelling. Moreover, as a matter of fact, most northern nationalists, including Sinn Féin supporters, prefer the option of shared authority to that of re-partition, which suggests that our argument is not merely an abstract one, divorced from popular feeling. In the JRRT/UMS polls referred to earlier 2 per cent of Sinn Féin supporters backed repartition as their first preference, and 9 per cent backed it as their second preference; by contrast 11 per cent of them backed the option most closely resembling shared authority as their first preference, and 20 per cent of them chose it as their second preference. [23] In short, if the first-preference of republicans cannot be satisfied, namely a united Ireland, then the available evidence suggests that they would prefer shared authority to re-partition. We therefore believe that supporters of the republican movement, if not all republican activists, could be persuaded that shared authority is an improvement on the status quo and that it is a fair compromise, rather than a unilateral defeat for nationalist objectives.

Fairness for Unionists

5.15. An obvious reaction to our argument so far might go as follows: while Irish and especially northern nationalists, including some militant republicans, might be persuaded of the fairness of shared authority unionists will not be at all sympathetic to it. We agree that a majority of unionists are not presently sympathetic to any alteration in indivisible British sovereignty over Northern Ireland. Indeed unionists object to the Anglo-Irish Agreement, amongst other reasons, because they think that it erodes British sovereignty. So how can the fairness of shared authority be made apparent to unionists ?

5.16. First of all we believe it is possible to show that the present normative position of many unionists is, like that of militant republicans, partial and unreasonable. They are committed to an illiberal theory of self-determination: in their philosophy only a majority, or as they usually say 'the majority', has the right to self-determination. 'The majority' for most unionists is not the majority within the United Kingdom as a whole, but rather the majority within Northern Ireland. However, most people, on reflection, agree that what

THE POSITIVE CASE 57

is sauce for the goose should also be sauce for the gander. If unionists maintain that the majority within the United Kingdom should not be able to over-rule the preferences of the majority within Northern Ireland then they must also concede that the majority within Northern Ireland has no right to over-rule the preferences of the minority within Northern Ireland. Majoritarian thinking cannot find a fair solution for Northern Ireland.* Many unionists go one step further: they do not believe that any part of Northern Ireland, let alone Northern Ireland itself, should have the right to secede from the United Kingdom.** They are committed either to the doctrine of 'one nation, one state', or to that of 'one people, one state'.*** However, unlike militant republicans, Ulster unionists have their illiberal version of self-determination presently enforced by British public law. We believe that the same argument we used to reject republican claims to a united

---

* A similar logic applies to nationalists: if they reject the right of a majority in Northern Ireland to impose its will on the minority they must logically accept that the nationalist majority in Ireland as a whole has no right to impose its will on the unionist minority in Ireland as a whole.
** However, *in extremis*, some of them believe that Northern Ireland should have the right to become independent. Some even hold to the apparently contradictory position of seeking the unqualified and permanent integration of Northern Ireland into the United Kingdom while suggesting that Northern Ireland should have the right to become independent. This contradiction can be reconciled - such unionists prefer integration but would rather have independence than see the unification of Ireland.
*** Arthur Aughey, a leading unionist political philosopher, maintains that unionists are not British nationalists but rather are (inarticulate) devotees of a liberal theory of citizenship of the democratic state (A. Aughey *Under Siege: Ulster Unionism and the Anglo-Irish Agreement* (London, Hurst, 1989). We do not accept Aughey's thesis that unionists are not British nationalists. We think (a) that is what most of them say they are, (b) that that is what they mean when they say 'Ulster is British', and (c) that it is possible to be a British nationalist while insisting on an Irish cultural identity.

However, even if one were to concede Aughey's claim and regard unionists as non-nationalists they are still 'sovereigntists', i.e. committed to the doctrine of indivisible sovereignty expressed in one state's authority. Proof of this trait can be found in the widespread hostility to European integration within the unionist community (which, as a matter of fact, mirrors that found in republican arguments against European integration).

Ireland as of right is equally compelling in rejecting the claim of Ulster unionists that Northern Ireland should be exclusively subject to British sovereignty. A liberal theory of self-determination not only excludes the republican case for a unified Ireland but also the unionist case for unqualified British sovereignty over Northern Ireland.

5.17. Secondly, we believe it is possible to defend the thesis that shared authority, as we envisage it, is equally fair to both communities, unionists as much as nationalists. To be fair shared authority must not be weighted against one community. On our proposals each national community is equally represented through the appointment of one member of the SACNI determined by their national head of government, while the Northern Ireland electorate chooses three members (a majority) of the SACNI, as well as choosing the APNI. We believe that the model we outlined in Chapter 4 achieves the goal of fairness, without sacrificing competitive democratic principles; and we will happily amend our proposals if readers can demonstrate that they are unbalanced and if they can suggest ways of making it fairer. Unionists may maintain that our model of shared authority will mark a shift towards nationalist objectives and therefore is biased towards 'the minority'. We maintain that while shared authority will indeed mark the achievement of legitimate constitutional nationalist objectives, it will also mark the achievement of legitimate unionist aspirations. Each community will be able to have its nationalist aspirations satisfied without doing so at the expense of the other. *Moreover, and more importantly, we maintain that if a model of shared authority is justifiable now, when Irish nationalists are a political minority within Northern Ireland, it would be equally justified if and when Irish nationalists become a political majority within Northern Ireland.* In other words durable shared authority can and must protect the present majority and minority *and* the possible future majority and minority in exactly the same way. If it does not, if a model of shared authority was defended and implemented as a short-run transitional step towards a united Ireland it would not be fair - and also would not be stable. Developing shared authority simply as a staging post to a united Ireland would simply invert the status quo. That is why the model of shared authority outlined in Chapter 4 makes it clear that we are advocating durable shared authority. * While we advocate leaving

---

* Under the proposal outlined in paragraph 4.20 Northern Ireland's status can only be changed with the support of three quarters of the electorate. It is clear why this proposal is balanced, because (a) the shift to shared authority from the status quo protects the present minority and (b) the proposed means of constitutional change protects

THE POSITIVE CASE 59

both communities free to negotiate an agreed future, different from that of shared authority, we do so in a way which guarantees that each community's right to self-determination is equally protected. We are convinced that shared authority will make the emergence of a broad political consensus between the two communities much more likely, but the content of that consensus is not for us to prescribe.

5.18. Thirdly, we believe that even when unionists' present preferences about the future of Northern Ireland are taken into account it can be shown that our model of shared authority is consistent with a reasonable compromise. When asked, unionists presently prefer the unqualified Union to an independent Northern Ireland. They also prefer an independent Northern Ireland to joint sovereignty.* This simplified account of their preference-structures suggests that for unionists a model of shared authority would be their third preference, whereas for republicans shared authority would be their second preference. However, it does not follow, for four reasons, that our proposal is biased towards republicans' preferences at the expense of unionists' preferences:

- First, *our model of shared authority, when examined closely, is in fact a synthesis of joint sovereignty and independence*, so it is in fact a compromise between the second preferences of hard-line unionists and republicans. Our model of shared authority, outlined below, permits maximum feasible agreed autonomy for Northern Ireland within a framework of co-sovereignty.

- Second, if the peoples of Northern Ireland agree, subject to the conditions outlined in paragraph 4.20, our model of shared authority also enables them to create a fully independent Northern Ireland - if there is widespread support for that idea within both communities. We emphasise, however, that while they are enabled to move towards independence under our model, they are not required to do so.**

---

equally any future unionist minority from a shift from the new status quo to a united Ireland. By contrast, some might argue that Northern Ireland's constitutional status should be capable of being changed with the support of a majority of the electorate (as at present). We disagree: simple majoritarianism caused the Northern Ireland conflict and will not resolve it.

* See Chapter 6. §18.1.
** The Anglo-Irish Agreement does not envisage that the peoples of Northern Ireland have the right to opt for independence - under Article

- Third, unionist advocacy of independence in preference to shared authority is subject to two significant objections:
  - Independence, unlike shared authority is not economically attractive, to put matters in the mildest possible way - at least if those advocating independence intend to preserve anything like existing living standards in the region .*
  - If unionists are to be free to seek independence rather than accept shared authority it would not follow, on the liberal theory of self-determination which we outlined above, that they would be justified in making all of Northern Ireland independent. On the logic outlined above only territories in which the overwhelming bulk of the population favoured independence would be entitled to secede from the Union. In other words the logic of a fair form of independence points inexorably towards a very messy re-partition of Northern Ireland - to which there are compelling counter-objections. **

  These two considerations provide forceful practical and liberal arguments against unionists who would seek to suggest that independence would be fairer than shared authority.

- Fourth, we believe independence is advocated by most unionists not as a positive alternative but rather because they believe it is their last-ditch response to the threat of a united Ireland. They prefer independence to joint authority primarily because they see the latter as a stepping stone to a united Ireland. It therefore follows that if they can be persuaded that shared authority is *not* a stepping stone to a united Ireland, but in fact makes the creation of a unified Ireland subject to a broader level of consent than is required under the status quo then our model is not vulnerable to the criticism that it is biased unfairly towards a nationalist agenda. For this reason unionists have good grounds to look at our proposals, especially that outlined in paragraph 4.20, with a less jaundiced eye: our model protects unionists much better against their worst-case scenario - a united Ireland - than they are presently protected under the status quo. Northern Ireland can now become part of the Republic of Ireland by a simple majority of the vote within Northern Ireland (Article 1 of the Anglo-Irish Agreement). This possibility is theoretically feasible within our lifetimes because of demographic changes and increased

---

1 they have the right to remain within the United Kingdom *or* to become part of the Republic of Ireland.
*   See Chapter 6. § 13.5.
**   See Chapter 6.§ 16 ff.

nationalism within the present minority community. We think that there should be a much more testing threshold of consent for a unified Ireland. Under our model of shared authority Northern Ireland could become exclusively part of the Republic of Ireland only with the support of three quarters of the electorate in Northern Ireland. For this reason under our model unionists will undoubtedly be better protected against their worst-case outcome than they are at present.* Unionists' worst-case scenario is republicans' first-preference, and we are proposing making the latter more difficult to accomplish by consent. It should therefore be apparent that our model is a fairer compromise from the perspective of unionists than might at first glance appear to be the case. The proof of this argument is that many nationalists will find this feature of our model its most objectionable element.

5.19 Our model of shared authority is a fair method of conflict-resolution. It takes each national community's preferences, interests and identities as they are, and not as others would like them to be, and seeks to establish that they can be equitably reconciled without letting one set triumph at the expense of the other. Each national community and its nation-state is to be put on an equal constitutional and institutional footing. Compared with the status quo our model offers much more substantive equality for northern nationalists and much

---

*   Unionists and people sympathetic to unionists complain that under the Anglo-Irish Agreement consent for a united Ireland merely requires 'a mathematical majority, and not a broad political consensus' - Cadogan Group *Northern Limits: Boundaries of the Attainable in Northern Ireland Politics* (Belfast, 1992), p. 24. This complaint makes sense to us, but it has two reciprocal corollaries which its authors fail to observe. First, the present Union is based on a mathematical local majority, *not* upon a broad political consensus in Northern Ireland, let alone the island of Ireland. Since the Cadogan Group implicitly believes that the status quo is defensible on a mathematical majority what grounds has it for opposing the idea that change in Northern Ireland's status should be determined by a simple mathematical majority ? Second, if sovereignty over Northern Ireland was shared in the future, and change from that status required a broad political consensus, then both communities and identities would be on an equal footing, and equally constitutionally respected, and not threatened by simple mathematical majorities, as both are at present. Our proposal for change in Northern Ireland's constitutional status after shared authority is established, as outlined in paragraph 4.20, is consistently against simple mathematical majorities.

greater long-term security for unionists.[24] The peoples of Northern Ireland are to be co-authors of their fate, together with the two governments of their preferred nation-states. This co-authorship extends to the future of Northern Ireland. The peoples of Northern Ireland will be free, subject to broad consensual requirements, to change the status of Northern Ireland - in any direction of their choice under the proposal outlined in paragraph 4.20. The just compromise embedded in this model is also compatible with accountable, representative and economically viable government.

Accountable and Representative Democratic Government

5.20. Sharing authority, responsibility and power are compatible with liberal democratic norms of participation and accountability, as we have shown in institutional detail in Chapter 4. Moreover, our model of shared authority has built-in 'democratic multipliers' to encourage political accommodation between the two major communities in Northern Ireland. If their representatives work this model successfully then this trust can lead to a switch from a separation-of-powers regime to a parliamentary system; and if the model works then the peoples of Northern Ireland can take shared control of their political, cultural and economic destinies; and if it works well they can assume full control of their own security. Our constitutional model has been designed to ensure that each community can have proportional representation in political institutions, self-government on cultural matters, and constitutional safeguards to protect its identity and interests.

5.21. The system we propose suggests a collective executive for Northern Ireland, composed of a majority of members elected by the citizens of Northern Ireland, and an assembly elected exclusively by the citizens of Northern Ireland. Our model ensures very extensive self-government for the peoples of Northern Ireland, while remaining consistent with Northern Ireland's proposed dual status. Together with the representatives of the British and Irish governments the members of the SACNI will be politically and electorally accountable for their actions. The British and Irish nominees will be accountable to their sovereign parliaments, and the peoples of Northern Ireland will be represented in the second chambers (at Westminster and Leinster House) of the external co-sovereigns.

5.22. We have proposed a formal separation of powers in Northern Ireland, i.e. we have separated the election, appointment and running of the executive, assembly and supreme court. This separation of

THE POSITIVE CASE 63

powers is accompanied by essential checks and balances to provide both principal communities with constitutional security.

- The mechanisms governing elections to the executive and assembly enable the executive and the assembly to reflect changes in public opinion, but also respect the principle of proportionality.*

- Elections for the executive (within Northern Ireland) and the assembly will take place under proportional representation; and the assembly will have a committee system which in its composition and chairships will respect the principle of proportionality.**

- The Shared Authority Council of Northern Ireland (the SACNI) has sufficient authority and power to be an effective executive, especially in conditions of emergency, but it is prevented from becoming an instrument of tyranny by
  (i) provisions requiring unanimity on proposals affecting national or religious rights and freedoms;
  (ii) the fact that it is a multi-person executive, staffed by people representing different constituencies.

- The Assembly of the Peoples of Northern Ireland (the APNI) is carefully designed to be representative in its composition and proportional in its functioning***; it has genuine powers of scrutiny and oversight; and it has the ability to expand its powers and capacities should there be widespread agreement to facilitate such developments.

- The mechanisms we have proposed to govern appointments to the Supreme Court respect the existence of co-sovereignty, and the

---

* The size of the APNI will ensure that it will be more broadly representative of public opinion than the SACNI (with its three elected representatives), but to ensure re-election, and to ease co-operation with the Assembly, the elected members of the SACNI will find it prudent to be responsive to changing opinion on matters of public policy and to shifts in party support within the APNI.
** In this respect our proposals can be considered a compromise between the SDLP's insistence that there be a system of shared authority, involving a collective executive in which the Irish government is represented, and the UUP and DUP's insistence that any assembly for Northern Ireland should be governed by the principle of proportionality, rather than that of compulsory power-sharing.
*** See the discussion of the Saint-Laguë rule in Appendix B.

principles of proportionality, and ensure that Northern Ireland will have an autonomous legal personality.

• The proposed Bill of Rights protects individual human rights, subject to explicit constitutional provisions to protect proportionality in public institutions, to rectify unjustified inequalities, and to enable each national community to protect its own cultural, educational and religious heritage without state interference.

• The proposed Constitution entrenches Northern Ireland's dual status as part of the United Kingdom and the Republic of Ireland, and ensures that each national community has constitutional safeguards against any proposals to change that status.

The principles of representative government, proportionality, the separation of powers, the Bill of Rights, the protection of fundamental national and religious rights and freedoms, and the dual status of Northern Ireland as defined in its Constitution, are all ingredients of a unified constitutional vision. They will combine to facilitate pluralist democratic government and block the possibility that any community will not have its interests represented, or be subject to control by a simple popular majority in Northern Ireland (either now or in the future).

Security

5.23. Under our model of shared authority each community obtains constitutional security, legal security, and policing security. These types of security are linked. Without constitutional and legal security - protecting fundamental rights and freedoms - each community will continue to generate paramilitant activists. Through the establishment of widely legitimate legal and policing institutions our model proposes mechanisms to diminish the support for and the capacities of the paramilitaries. We have already outlined our mechanisms for establishing widely legitimate legal institutions in our proposed Bill of Rights, protections for fundamental national and religious rights and freedoms, Supreme Court, Directorate of Public Prosecutions, and proposals for the functioning of courts handling 'certified in' scheduled offences.* We must now address the critical issues of establishing legitimate policing and providing military support to the civil power.

---

* Our proposed legal institutions are fully elaborated in Chapter 4.

5.24. Any worthwhile proposal for the future of Northern Ireland must address, consistent with the rule of law, the issues raised by policing a divided society. Such a proposal must be both realistic and democratic. While we believe that shared authority will ultimately remove the root causes of paramilitarism in both communities, we would not expect it to lead to an immediate and complete cessation in violence. Indeed, in the short term, the prospects of continuing (or an upsurge in both) loyalist and republican violence must be considered probable rather than possible. However, any proposal sufficiently radical to tackle the underlying political problems of Northern Ireland runs the same risk. We believe that this risk is worth taking, in part because our proposals provide for the containment and eventual cessation of paramilitarism.

Political Control, Accountability and Legitimacy

5.25. Political control of security policy must be the responsibility of the new institutions established under shared authority.* Unionists resent the present lack of control over security policy by Northern Ireland's elected representatives. Our proposals would eventually remedy this deficiency. However, we recognise that there will be some difficulties in moving quickly towards this objective. Given their past experiences, northern nationalists have less faith in locally controlled security forces than they do in the British Army, and institutional memories of the 1960s and 1970s have left both the British and Irish governments suspicious of regional control over security.

5.26. Mechanisms need to be established which reflect these legitimate fears, while also opening up the possibility of regional democratic involvement in security. We therefore propose that security policy should be initially the shared responsibility of the British and Irish nominated members of the Shared Authority Council for Northern Ireland. However, provision should be made for a three stage process in which Northern Ireland's representatives can be gradually integrated into security policy:

---

* It would be sensible for a committee consisting of the British Home Secretary, the Irish Minister for Justice, and two members of the SACNI, to co-ordinate security co-operation across and within the three jurisdictions. Initially, as outlined in the next paragraph in the text, the two members of the SACNI serving on this committee would be the British and Irish nominees.

- in the first instance security policy will be the responsibility of the nominated members of the SACNI;

- then the elected members of the SACNI and the relevant Northern Ireland ministers can be brought into the appropriate security policy-making committees of the SACNI; and

- finally an Assembly committee will be consulted on and be able to scrutinise security policy.

This three-stage process will be consistent with the 'democratic multiplier' effect to which we have previously referred. *

5.27. As with all existing political institutions in Northern Ireland, the major difficulty confronting the present security forces, the Royal Ulster Constabulary, the British Army, and the Royal Irish Regiment, is their lack of legitimacy in the eyes of large sections of the nationalist community. Their acceptability is undermined by their role managing conflict 'at the frontiers' of a divided society, and the predominantly Protestant and British identities of their personnel.** We believe that legitimising the security forces in the eyes of the communities which presently treat them with hostility or suspicion would greatly enhance their ability to deal with paramilitary violence - far more than any increase in their resources, or any extensions in anti-terrorism legislation. The security forces themselves would derive substantial advantages from the creation of legitimate political institutions which

---

* In the second stage we envisage the SACNI appointing a five person police committee, in which each member is nominated by one member of the SACNI.
** There is accumulating evidence that the RUC is regarded with suspicion by sections of the unionist community. We note that some nationalists take comfort from the fact that the RUC now has vocal unionist critics. Indeed, there are people in the security establishment who see this development as a sign of the RUC's greater professionalism, and argue that nationalists should therefore be more sympathetic to the RUC. We believe that this thinking shows the awful consequences of zero-sum politics: the capacity of the RUC to alienate sections of both communities on an impartial basis is hardly a constructive solution to the problems of policing without consent. While it is clearly unhelpful if one community regards the RUC as its property, it is even less helpful if neither community regards it as an institution which will uphold the rule of law, impartially, and with respect for human rights.

guaranteed the fundamental rights and national identities of both unionists and nationalists, and ensured equitable participation in government for both traditions.

The RUC and the Northern Ireland Police Service

5.28. Many people, including serving RUC officers, believe that the RUC must be reformed so that police organisation in Northern Ireland respects the principles of fairness, proportionality and genuine security - the ingredients identified in our arguments for shared authority.* However, such reforms cannot simply be confined to the changes in procedures and codes of practices that one could anticipate members of the SACNI wishing to introduce. Structural reforms are evidently necessary if both communities are to identify equally with the police. Despite very welcome improvements in the professionalism of the RUC, and its increasing reputation for impartiality (at least in the view of outsiders), which gives us confidence in its capacities to deal with the initial phases of shared authority, it nevertheless remains an organisation considered alien and oppressive by many nationalists, including large numbers of constitutional nationalists who are bitterly opposed to the IRA.

5.29. At a political level, the negative image of the police force will be gradually changed by ensuring that the police are seen to be defending political and legal institutions in which elected representatives of both traditions are represented and respected. Shared authority will achieve these objectives, and constitutional nationalist leaders would then have sufficient confidence and authority unequivocally to encourage their supporters to endorse and join the police force. However, this latter issue raises a very practical concern. There is a pressing need for a major medium and long-term increase in the number of police officers recruited from the nationalist community - itself a symptom of Northern Ireland's divided past and present. This need is already recognised by the RUC but for a variety of obvious reasons - including the present political status of Northern Ireland, IRA attacks on the security forces, and the biased image of the police - its success in recruiting such officers has been limited.

5.30. We believe that if policing is eventually to function in harmony with the new political structures, the establishment of a new police

---

* While we recognise that the existing security forces have prevented many acts of violence, they have not succeeded in providing acceptable levels of security for the peoples of Northern Ireland.

organisation will become necessary. It should have a new and more neutral name, the Northern Ireland Police Service (NIPS)*, and it should consist of existing RUC officers wishing to transfer to the NIPS, new recruits drawn from both communities, and initially should also include temporarily seconded members of British police forces and members of the Gárda Síochána - at all levels, depending on operational requirements. The latter would be particularly important in providing officers from an Irish nationalist background sufficiently experienced to occupy senior posts - until such time as there are reasonable numbers of locally recruited nationalists in a position to compete effectively for promotion to senior positions. Within three years of the establishment of shared authority the SACNI should set targets and timetables to ensure that the Northern Ireland Police Service becomes socially representative.

5.31. The preceding argument suggests that the principle of a regional police organisation corresponds most closely with the type of political institutions we propose. For the time being we believe that the idea of creating local community police forces, which would be involved in anti-paramilitary activities, poses far too many overt difficulties. However, we do not rule out the possibility that the SACNI and the Assembly of the Peoples of Northern Ireland might at some future juncture consider it appropriate to reorganise the police force along the lines of a more decentralised model, or indeed divide functional responsibilities so that the NIPS can concentrate on policing major crimes against the person while local forces would be responsible for other policing tasks.

5.32. While we have suggested that it is important to retain a Northern Ireland wide police service we are nevertheless convinced that it would be sensible if officers were operationally deployed to take into account the composition of the communities they police. Any inflexibility, or internal rivalries within the service, which might result from the implementation of this principle would be outweighed by the

---

* Before the Opsahl Commission one witness asked the question 'Why does Northern Ireland have a "royal" police force, a recognisable instrument of the state, when the rest of the UK has regional police forces ?' (cited in Pollak, A. (ed.), *A Citizens' Inquiry*, op.cit. p. 62.) In addition to calling the police the Northern Ireland Police Force it might also be appropriate to consider giving it an additional and specifically Gaelic title.

THE POSITIVE CASE 69

consequent gains in legitimacy and public co-operation.* For example, the existing RUC, drawn predominantly from the unionist community, has generally been more successful in bringing loyalist paramilitaries to justice than in dealing with the IRA and other republican paramilitary organisations. This facet of the RUC's capabilities has been demonstrated in its better clear-up rate for killings carried out by loyalist paramilitaries. We think it is reasonable to assume that extensive nationalist participation in the NIPS would ensure its effectiveness against any republican paramilitary activity.

5.33. The RUC belongs to the tradition of quasi-military police forces introduced into Ireland by the Peace Preservation Act of 1814 and the Ireland (Constabulary) Act of 1836 - which established the Royal Irish Constabulary, the precursor of the RUC. This tradition of quasi-military policing is in stark contrast to the civilian policing style of Great Britain and independent Ireland. Despite the fact that the Hunt Report of 1969 recommended that the RUC be reconstructed as an unarmed civilianised police force it has remained a quasi-military organisation - albeit for reasons which have not altogether been within its control.** We regretfully accept that in the transition to shared authority the RUC will have to remain armed, and that its successor, the new Northern Ireland Police Service, will of necessity begin its life as an armed organisation.*** However, the legislation establishing the NIPS should make it clear that it is only to be armed to the extent that there is a paramilitary threat to security within Northern Ireland. The right of the NIPS to bear arms on a routine basis should therefore be subject to periodic approval by the Shared Authority Council for

---

* Organisational rhetoric which suggests that 'when a person puts on his or her uniform, he or she is no longer a Protestant or a Catholic, British or Irish, but simply a police officer or a soldier' forgets that the people being policed cannot, for the time being, see matters in the same light.
** See the Hunt Report, *Report of the Advisory Committee on Police in Northern Ireland* (Belfast, Cmd. 535). The Report also recommended the disbandment of the notorious Ulster Special Constabulary (the 'B Specials') and outlined proposals for what would eventually emerge as the Ulster Defence Regiment.
*** The Government of the Irish Free State established the Civic Guard, which became the Gárda Síochána, as an unarmed police force during the Irish Civil War. However, because of the protracted nature of the conflict in Northern Ireland, amongst other reasons, we do not think it would be possible to repeat such a radical experiment in Northern Ireland.

Northern Ireland. Indeed, the extent to which the NIPS can disarm itself should be taken as an index of its success in establishing its public legitimacy. Above all, it must be made clear that the NIPS is not committed to the quasi-military traditions of the RIC and RUC, and its initiation marks a decisive step towards bringing policing in Northern Ireland into line with the pattern in Great Britain and the Republic.

5.34. We recognise that the short term loyalist or republican response to shared authority might well mean an escalation in political violence. Providing for this contingency would no doubt require a temporary and conventional build-up of security force personnel. However, we believe the Irish authorities should also directly participate in the defence of the new institutions. In particular, officers from the Gárda Síochána should be seconded to the RUC to assist in anti-paramilitary activities, particularly at senior level. Moreover, we recognise that provision must be made for military assistance for the Shared Authority Council of Northern Ireland.

Military Assistance to the Civil Power

5.35. As long as significant paramilitary activity continues, it is likely that the RUC, or its successor, the Northern Ireland Police Service, will require military assistance. In line with the principles of shared authority we believe that the police service, with the approval of the political authorities responsible for security, should have the power to call on the British and Irish armed forces for assistance in areas or in operations where it cannot act alone.

5.36. We would expect the authorities to ensure that any such military deployments took into account the nature of the local community or communities. For example, we would not expect to see Irish Army units patrolling in Larne, and we would not think it an efficient or rational use of resources to maintain the large-scale British Army presence in Crossmaglen.

5.37. The primacy of the civilian authorities over the military organisations must be upheld. The new political authorities, at least initially, would clearly have to involve themselves more deeply in the operations of the security forces than has been the case since 1971-2. Similarly, the new NIPS, supported by the SACNI, would have to demonstrate its tight supervision of military assistance. While military organisations have understandable reasons for wishing to preserve their autonomy, there have been too many occasions in Northern Ireland when the effects of such autonomy have not been conducive to public order, or respect for the rule of law. In short the NIPS should have a veto on army operations and on deployment decisions.

5.38. In addition, a committee of the SACNI and the NIPS should have the final say on recruitment and retention in the (Northern Ireland only) battalions of the Royal Irish Regiment (RIR), and on the areas and tasks for which it is deployed. In any case, we believe that the eventual reduction in paramilitary activity resulting from the implementation of shared authority will lessen the need for the RIR to remain on active service in Northern Ireland. In the event of the termination of the paramilitary threat the RIR shall be demobilised and its members offered employment in British or Irish army regiments. In the meantime we believe that the RIR should be re-named, perhaps as the Northern Ireland Defence Force, and perform the functions intended for its predecessor, the Ulster Defence Regiment, i.e. it should function as a static defence force, protecting public buildings and installations, and not participate in military patrols or operations. It will be under the clear operational guidance of the NIPS. The essential elements of our proposed security system for Northern Ireland are summarised in Figure 5.1.

Economic Feasibility

5.39. To complete our case for sharing authority, responsibility and power we must show why we believe our model is not only compatible with principles of fiscal equity and accountability, but also consistent with the economic interests of all the parties concerned.

Monetary Institutions

5.40. Since it is our objective to establish a model of shared authority which synthesises the advantages of joint authority and independence we believe that the economic arrangements which best match our arguments would involve granting Northern Ireland maximum feasible economic autonomy - consistent with the protection of national and religious rights and freedoms. This logic suggests that Northern Ireland should have its own currency, with its value set in the normal way, together with the freedom to tax and spend its own resources, and complete freedom to set its own budget-deficits. This option would maximise the responsibility enjoyed by local political agents, and the effective choices of citizens expressing their preferences in elections. This logic would also have the great advantage of reducing the economic points of friction which might otherwise complicate British-

72 THE POSITIVE CASE

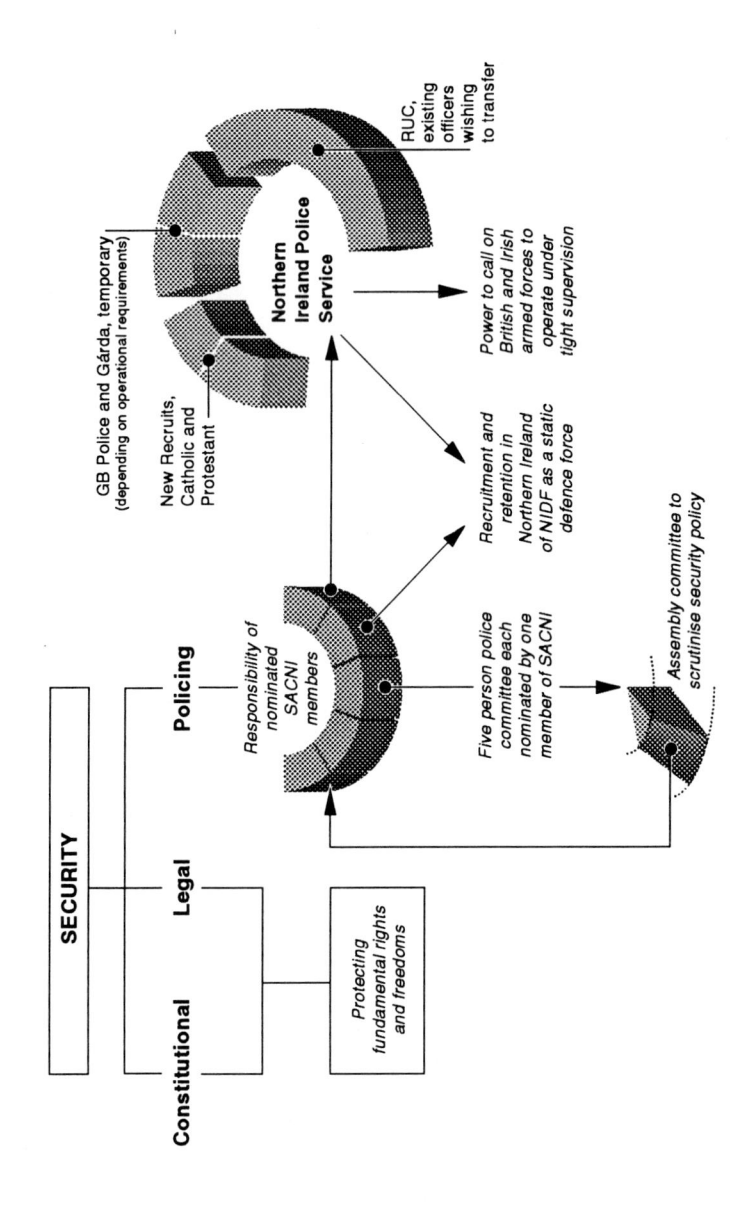

Figure 5.1

Irish, Irish-Northern Irish, and British-Northern Irish relations. It would mean that neither Britain nor the Republic would have to act as guarantors of Northern Ireland's debt, and would obviate the need for them to act as joint guarantors of debt - which would be institutionally messy, given that the two countries will usually have different credit ratings. It would also mean that the SACNI, together with the APNI, would possess the full armoury of economic policy-making powers, and could seek to rectify structural disadvantages which have restrained economic development in Northern Ireland. They could, for example, seek to change the real exchange rate to their advantage. Under this option Northern Ireland would have its own currency, and its own central bank. The currency would not be rigidly tied to either the pound sterling or the Irish *punt*, but would exchange at a rate determined by market conditions and the monetary and fiscal policies pursued by the Central Bank and the Minister of Finance. The Central Bank would be entitled to an annual fiduciary issue of notes, set by statute at the equivalent of, say, £200 million indexed to local GDP one year in arrears. This policy would allow the Northern Ireland authorities to finance a useful, but strictly limited amount of public expenditure through note-issue rather than through taxes or borrowing. It could be decided that note-issues above an agreed fiduciary level would have to be fully backed by Northern Ireland Central Bank deposits with either the Bank of England or the Bank of Ireland - converted into the relevant currency at the current exchange rate. (This restriction would prevent excessive monetary creation and help preserve confidence in the Northern Ireland currency.)

5.41. While we believe in the abstract validity of the logic outlined above we realise that serious transitional difficulties are attached to establishing an economically autonomous Northern Ireland. To begin with there is considerable uncertainty surrounding the question of European monetary union. If European monetary union is rapidly realised then there is little point in pursuing the institutional disruption which would be occasioned by Northern Ireland developing its own currency and central bank. Therefore we would propose that the move towards economic autonomy for Northern Ireland be postponed until the question of European monetary union is resolved. If European monetary union does not occur by 1999 the SACNI should be left free to establish Northern Ireland's economic autonomy. This decision leaves us with the matter of what transitional arrangements should be pursued. In the light of uncertainty surrounding the future of British and Irish exchange rates there are two possible options which might be followed within a system of shared authority:

- Under option 1, the simplest option, Northern Ireland's currency would remain the pound sterling. This option would cause the least disruption, and would have a sound economic rationale: presently Northern Ireland's trade with Great Britain is more extensive than its trade with the Republic.

- Under option 2, Northern Ireland's currency would become the Irish *punt*. This option would encourage harmonisation across all of Ireland, but would cause disruption. Moreover, the present commitment of the Republic to the European Monetary System might or might not have severe deflationary implications for Northern Ireland. We therefore believe that it would not be prudent to pursue this option in the foreseeable future.

We believe that until the issue of European monetary union is resolved it would be prudent to pursue option 1.

Budgetary Issues

5.42. Under our model of shared authority it is intended that spending and taxation decisions should be taken primarily by elected representatives from Northern Ireland in the SACNI, scrutinised and possibly amended by the APNI. We believe that it would be most desirable, whether or not Northern Ireland has full monetary autonomy, for the region to enjoy full fiscal autonomy. Moreover, we believe that a responsible SACNI should be enabled to borrow money to fund public expenditure and pay its own interest rates on such loans. This step would enable decision-makers to manage the economy responsibly. The alternative policy would be to let fiscal and expenditure decisions be subject to clear budgetary guidelines, determined jointly by Britain and the Irish Republic, setting out the region's entitlements regarding external aid and its ability to raise money by borrowing. Under these arrangements loans to Northern Ireland would be guaranteed by the external powers, primarily Britain but also the Irish Republic. In these circumstances there would be an obvious temptation for the SACNI and the APNI to borrow excessively in the hope that the external powers would ultimately foot the bill. To avoid this danger explicit limits would have to be placed on the extent of local deficit financing, and on the region's ability to accumulate debt. (There is an obvious parallel here with the restrictions envisaged under the Maastricht Agreement, which are intended to prevent excessive borrowing by European governments in the uncertain event that monetary union should occur). We would prefer to give the SACNI full fiscal and expenditure responsibility for the local economy - excluding expenditures on security forces provided by the external co-sovereigns - but we recognise that unless Northern Ireland enjoys full economic autonomy limitations have to be placed on its capacity to incur debt.

5.43. The fact that Northern Ireland might receive a given amount of aid from outside the region should not, in our view, determine how this money should be spent. Presently, apart from security expenditure, most public spending and taxation in Northern Ireland are determined by the principle that tax rates and welfare entitlements should be the same as in Great Britain. However, there is no reason why this principle should continue to be the case under shared authority. Within the framework of a given amount of outside aid, it would be better for Northern Ireland's politicians to be free to vary tax and spending according to local conditions and preferences, rather than simply following priorities laid down in Westminster, as at present. For example, the electorate in Northern Ireland might wish to raise taxes to finance greater public spending, and reflect that wish through its voting for candidates for the SACNI and the APNI. Or it might wish to do the opposite. In either case, it can only be healthy that the peoples of Northern Ireland, and their representatives, should have the opportunity to make, or at least strongly influence, such decisions. One of the main reasons why politics in Northern Ireland is so sterile is that virtually nothing of practical importance is presently decided by elected bodies, with the result that elections are often little more than symbolic plebiscites on the border and related issues. Under our proposals local politicians will have real influence over the major public expenditure and taxation decisions, and co-operation across the national and sectarian divide would become a practical necessity. With important economic issues at stake, divisions would open up within each community and cross-community alliances on particular issues would develop. We are not, however, naïve: communal politics would not disappear, but some of the present antagonisms might be softened by the experience of co-operation over common policy objectives.

5.44. After their experience of the old Stormont regime, Catholics and northern nationalists may be worried that any provision for local control over public spending and taxation would be exploited in a discriminatory fashion. However, under our model of shared authority there would be powerful safeguards against such abuse. Spending and taxation decisions would be supervised by the SACNI, which would include at a minimum one Irish governmental representative, and one northern nationalist, and such decisions would also be subject to challenge in the courts, to ensure they were not biased towards any particular community. It must also be recalled that demographic trends are undermining Protestants' numerical majority and that a significant number of Protestants support the anti-sectarian Alliance party. Given these political realities, and the built-in constitutional safeguards in our model, we believe that local control over spending and taxation could not be seriously abused for sectarian purposes.

The Subvention, Aid, and Sharing the Burden

5.45. Any analysis of the future options for Northern Ireland must recognise that presently the region's economic performance is very unsatisfactory, and that the living standards of its peoples are heavily externally subsidised - by British and European tax-payers. [25] As with many other industrial regions elsewhere in Europe the Northern Ireland manufacturing sector has undergone a radical contraction in the past two decades. However, this decline has been exacerbated by armed conflict which has scared off external investors who might otherwise have brought new enterprises and employment to the region.

5.46. The main source of external support for Northern Ireland is the British government, which is currently spending at least £ (UK) 3 billion a year more on the region than it collects in tax revenue.* The rising cost of the subvention of Northern Ireland is illustrated in Figure 5.2. The subvention has shot up dramatically during the present slump, though it will probably fall back again when there is an economic recovery in the UK, and when tax increases or spending cuts are implemented. Part of the external support accrues automatically through the normal mechanisms of civilian welfare spending on health, education and social security benefits - entitlements to which the residents of Northern Ireland are presently entitled like other citizens of the UK. Indeed, in health and education expenditures per capita spending in Northern Ireland exceeds the UK average. The British government also channels in funds through its expenditures on the army, the police, and the prison service, commitments that have mushroomed during the present conflict. These security expenditures generate a great deal of employment and revenue in Northern Ireland - though these benefits are concentrated amongst Protestants and the unionist community who provide most of the local personnel employed in security.

---

* Data on the British "subvention" to Northern Ireland since 1966-67 are given in Appendix C. Appendices E-G present a brief statistical profile of the Northern Ireland economy together with some comparisons with Great Britain and the Republic of Ireland.

THE POSITIVE CASE 77

5.47. Another source of external support is the European Community, which supplies approximately £ (UK) 100 million a year under its own name to Northern Ireland, through special social, structural and other regional funds. It is also indirectly responsible for certain other transfers to Northern Ireland, especially payments under the Common Agricultural Policy, which are funnelled to Northern Ireland through Westminster and are officially classified as British governmental expenditure.

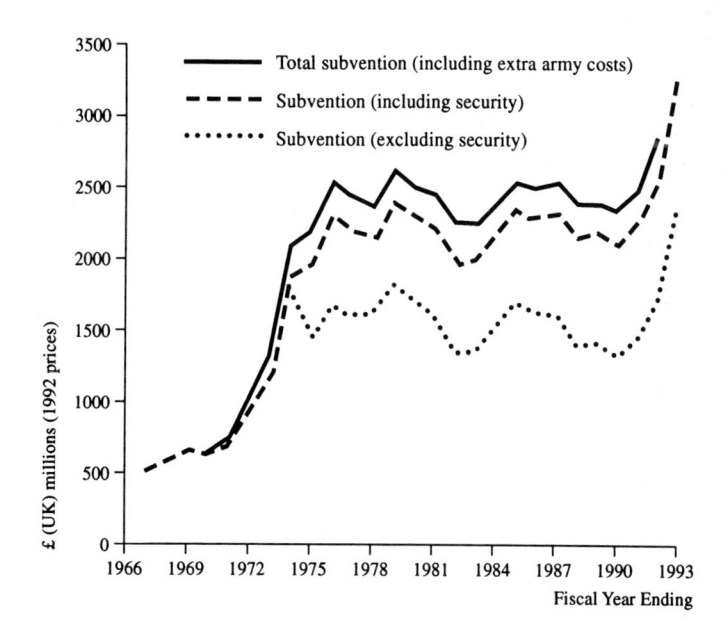

Figure 5.2. The UK Subvention of Northern Ireland
(1966/67 - 1992/93)
Source of data: Appendix C, data in 1992 prices.

5.48. Despite this extensive external support Northern Ireland has the highest unemployment rate and the lowest average level of personal consumption of any region in the UK. It also has by far the highest incidence of poverty. Poverty and unemployment are especially concentrated within the Catholic community, but are also common within the Protestant community.[26] Without external support, the standard of living would drop sharply, many jobs would disappear and there would be mass emigration from the region.[27] If external support was rapidly removed inter-communal strife would almost certainly intensify in the ensuing scramble for jobs. Any viable plan for shared authority in Northern Ireland must, therefore, accept that substantial aid will be required for many years to come. If peace can be restored, Northern Ireland may eventually become self-financing, but in the meantime it must be externally supported.

5.49. The amount of aid required for Northern Ireland depends both on what happens to the regional economy and on what target is set for the local standard of living. At present the economy is performing poorly (see Appendices E-G). Per capita output of private goods and services is about 64 per cent of the average in Great Britain, whilst personal consumption of such items is 82 per cent of the British average. External finance is partly used to bridge the gap between these two figures. It is also used to provide equipment and materials for the army, police, health, education and other public services.

5.50. Whether there is peace or war, the economy of Northern Ireland will remain weak for many years to come. The performance of local industry has improved recently and it has weathered the present slump comparatively well. But even under the most optimistic scenario, it will be at least a decade before the economy of Northern Ireland is strong enough to support the present relative standard of living in the region. To maintain this relative standard under shared authority, the total external cost must be assumed to be around £3 billion a year for the foreseeable future* - although we might expect the security element to fall with the success of shared authority. However, this is not the only option. One possibility would be to bring the standard of living in Northern Ireland gradually into line with that in the Irish Republic. However, personal consumption in the Republic is less than 60 per cent of the British average, compared with 84 per cent in Northern Ireland, and there is also a significant gap in the level of public services. Northern Ireland can enjoy a higher standard of living than the Republic simply because it receives such massive support from Britain. Even with no improvement in the Northern Ireland economy, if earnings, taxation and social expenditures in Northern Ireland were gradually harmonised with those in the Republic, the amount of external aid required in the medium term would fall considerably, but such a policy would be bitterly resented by both communities in Northern Ireland. We shall therefore take it that policy-

---

* This estimate includes security expenditure by the outside powers. The exact amount would depend on the security situation and on economic conditions. The figure given here assumes some reduction in security expenditure and some economic recovery in Northern Ireland.

makers should at least set themselves the more ambitious target of maintaining the present relative standard of living in Northern Ireland until such time as the region is ready for economic autonomy.

5.51. Who is to provide the money required to support Northern Ireland under a system of shared authority, pending the establishment of economic autonomy ? Part of the cost of supporting the region is already met by the European Community. However EC funds are scarce and claims on them are likely to mount as poorer East European countries queue up to join the European Union, so it would be unwise to expect significant extra funding from this quarter. The United States might provide some additional aid, but just how much is unclear, and the same applies to the states which have contributed to the International Fund for Ireland.

5.52. Therefore the bulk of financial support would almost certainly have to come from the two states sharing authority, namely Britain and the Republic of Ireland. In addition, the two states would have to meet certain military expenses which would not materially contribute to the local standard of living in Northern Ireland. These security expenses would include equipment for the army and police, together with pay for troops from the Republic and Great Britain engaged on security duties relating to Northern Ireland. Taking all types of expenditure into account, we shall assume that the total cost to the two countries combined would be £ (UK) 3 billion a year.

5.53. This burden could be divided between them in a variety of ways. Some illustrative calculations are shown in Table 5.1. Since the two states share authority over Northern Ireland equally, it could be argued that they should share equally in the cost of supporting the region. However, what constitutes 'equal sharing' ? One interpretation of equal sharing of the burden might be to suggest a simple 50:50 division of the total costs of supporting and policing the region. This rule would impose an unacceptable burden on the Irish Republic, which is a small and relatively poor country by comparison with Great Britain. The cost would amount to £ (UK) 428 per annum for every man, woman and child in the Republic, and would require an average reduction of almost 12 per cent in personal consumption.

5.54. A more just, sensible and realistic interpretation of 'equal sharing' is to follow the principle adopted by the United Nations and its subsidiary organisations, where all participating countries have the same voting rights but their financial contributions are based on their ability to pay.* The obvious measure of ability to pay is gross national product (GNP), which is equal to total domestic production plus net income from abroad in the form of interest, profits and dividends. This principle of burden-sharing would ensure that the weight of the burden would be equitably borne by British and Irish tax-payers. With contributions to the subvention made proportional to GNP the Irish Republic would have to provide £ (UK) 107 million per annum and Great Britain would have to provide £ (UK) 2893 million per annum. This rule would represent a cost of around 0.8 per cent of personal consumption in each country. Given that Britain is already spending this money, it would make no real difference to British tax-payers.

Table 5.1. Sharing the burden: some illustrative calculations

	£ million		£ per capita		% of GNP		% of personal consumption	
	IR	GB	IR	GB	IR	GB	IR	GB
A. Equal Division	1500	1500	428	27	8.6	0.3	11.8	0.4
B. Proportional to GNP	107	2893	31	52	0.6	0.6	0.8	0.8

Note: This table assumes that the total cost of supporting Northern Ireland is £ (UK) 3, 000 millions. Alternative rules for dividing this cost are illustrated.

5.55. What is insufficiently realised is that the Republic of Ireland presently faces a higher per capita burden from the conflict than Britain does. Moreover, with a fair system of 'equal sharing' of the burden under shared authority, the Republic would face little or no increase in its present expenditures. At present, because of the conflict in and over

---

* Any consistent opponent of proportional contributions like that in our proposed model of shared authority should argue that Britain should lose its place as a permanent member of the Security Council of the United Nations - where Britain presently has co-equal voting rights with the USA, Russia, France and China, even though it does not make a contribution to the organisation of the same size as the other four members of the Security Council. Conversely, such a critic might argue that China (on a head-count of citizens) should have twenty times as many votes as Britain.

Northern Ireland, the Republic deploys extra soldiers and police in border areas, while Britain provides troops recruited in Great Britain, and also pays for police and soldiers locally recruited in Northern Ireland. Under shared authority there would be some transfer of security duties between the two countries, with forces from the Republic taking over some of the tasks now performed by British soldiers, and locally recruited soldiers. At present as a proportion of GNP the cost of security operations is much greater for the Republic than it is for Britain.* Under shared authority this imbalance would be greater. Therefore as and when the imbalance in security expenditure was taken into account, the amount of new explicit financial aid required from the Republic under shared authority would be negligible. The Republic's main expenditure on Northern Ireland would be the cost of meeting its security obligations.

5.56. There are two further issues regarding the subvention which need to be considered. The first concerns its durability. The subvention can *either* be considered as support for Northern Ireland in transition towards economic autonomy and responsibility *or* as a permanent amount of support fixed arbitrarily in real terms at present levels of British public policy commitments and present relativities in living standards. We cannot think of a good argument in equity or logic for the latter possibility, so we would favour the subvention being set with a view to being reviewed when Northern Ireland is ready for greater economic autonomy. The second issue concerns the freedom of the SACNI and the APNI to distribute the funds from the subvention. If they have complete virement then they will automatically incur the full costs of security expenditure: if security expenditure rises the subvention will not be increased as it will be fixed, albeit in real terms. On the other hand if they have partial virement (with some elements of the subvention exempted from local decision-making) one prudent budgetary idea would be to make Northern Ireland partially responsible for the cost of security. At present security activities in Northern

---

* 'Although the absolute security cost to the British Government of the violence in 1982/83 is estimated as three and a half times that of the Irish Government in 1982 the proportionate expenditure on a per capita basis was equivalent to £ (IR) 9 in the UK compared to £ (IR) 36 in the South' (New Ireland Forum, *The Cost of Violence arising from the Northern Ireland Crisis*, (Dublin: Stationary Office, 1984,) para 6.3 p. 10). In other words the Republic of Ireland spends four times as much *per capita* as the United Kingdom does on security related to Northern Ireland. This estimate was made just over ten years ago, but it is probably still reasonably accurate.

Ireland are externally financed and cost the local population virtually nothing. On the contrary a perverse incentive is at work: security expenditure by the British government brings a great deal of income and employment to the region, mainly, but not exclusively, to the Protestant community. This asymmetry creates the anomalous situation that in the short-run, at least, much of the region actually benefits from security expenditure and has no economic incentive to see it reduced, and, moreover, these benefits are concentrated in one community. We believe that under shared authority this perverse incentive-structure could be eliminated by creating an implicit security tax for the region. Such a scheme might work as follows. Suppose that Northern Ireland was required to pay a fixed proportion, say 40 per cent, of the total cost of security in the region. External aid would initially be set sufficiently high both to finance payment of this security 'tax' and to provide the target standard of living for the local population. It would then be announced that any future changes in security expenditure, positive or negative, would be reflected *pari passu* in the amount of security tax paid by Northern Ireland. The total volume of financial aid going to the region would not be affected by variations in the rate of security tax, so the full cost or benefit of these variations would accrue to the people of Northern Ireland. This fiscal regime would provide an incentive for co-operation between the two communities, since a major part of the resulting savings in security expenditure would be passed on to them for use as they pleased - either to cut local taxes or expand public services and social benefits. * This fiscal incentive would therefore work in harmony with our other 'democratic multipliers'.

Summary

5.57. In this chapter we have made our positive case for our model of shared authority. We have attempted to demonstrate that it is fair to unionists and nationalists; that it provides constitutional security and equality for both communities, and democratic rights of citizenship for individuals in Northern Ireland; that it is consistent with accountable, representative and responsible constitutional government; that it establishes a legitimate and effective security system and administration of justice; and, lastly, but not least, that it is consistent with an economic regime which can provide fiscal equity, share burdens fairly, maintain existing living standards, and provide incentives to encourage economic development and responsibility. In

---

* Specimen formulae showing how the subvention might be calculated are presented in Appendix D.

the next chapter we shall argue that our model of shared authority is superior to all the other major constitutional options for Northern Ireland.

CHAPTER 6. THE NEGATIVE CASE:
why sharing authority is better than the other options

6.1. Our argument should not be misconstrued. It is not intended to foreclose debate. Quite the contrary. We are not pretending that shared authority is the only possible way of making progress for the peoples of Northern Ireland, although we do believe it is the best way of doing so. Other options for the future of Northern Ireland have persuasive and sincere advocates, and in what follows we do not impugn the motives or suggest bad faith on the part of those whose proposals diverge from our own. Instead we aim to persuade the proponents of other views that a system of shared authority would be fairer, more feasible, democratically stable, and economically sustainable than the multiple rival options on offer.

6.2. We have not advocated shared authority out of blind enthusiasm, political expediency, or out of a perverse preference for intellectual and constitutional novelty, but because through argument and dialogue we have been collectively persuaded that shared authority is the best way forward for Northern Ireland. Our proposals are in many respects the outcome of debate flowing from considering the rival standpoints and treating them seriously.

The Three Big Questions: Which state ? Which form of territorial government ? Which strategy ?

6.3. We start from the supposition that all options for the future of Northern Ireland have to resolve three big issues: the statehood of the region, its territorial form of government, and the public policy framework (with respect to its national, ethnic and religious heritage) which will guide its institutions. [28] If the immediate likelihood of a European super-state is ruled out, then there are five ways in which Northern Ireland's statehood could be arranged now, or in the future, and there are three principal territorial forms through which Northern Ireland's statehood might be organised. Finally, there are two grand public policy strategies which might be pursued in the region.

    6.3.1. The five ways in which Northern Ireland's statehood could be resolved are as follows:
      (a) Northern Ireland could remain wholly part of the UK;
      (b) Northern Ireland could become wholly part of the Republic of Ireland;
      (c) Northern Ireland could become an independent state;

(d) Northern Ireland could be partitioned between the United Kingdom and the Republic of Ireland;
(e) Northern Ireland could, as we have suggested, become part of both the UK and the Republic of Ireland. *

6.3.2. The three ways in which Northern Ireland's territorial form of government could be resolved are as follows:
(i) Northern Ireland could be part of a unitary state, whether that state is the UK, the Republic, or an independent Northern Ireland;
(ii) Northern Ireland could be part of a federal state, whether that state is the UK, the Republic, or an independent Northern Ireland; **
(iii) Northern Ireland could be part of a confederation, whether that state is the UK, the Republic, or an independent Northern Ireland. ***

6.3.3. There are two public policy strategies which might be pursued in Northern Ireland:
(I) the objective of public policy might be to eliminate national, ethnic and religious difference, either through assimilation or integration, or though partition (or secession);
(II) the objective of public policy might alternatively be to accommodate national, ethnic and religious differences through institutional pluralism. ****

The resulting array of options for the future of Northern Ireland is displayed in Table 6.1. It is capable of further variation and permutation, but presents the major proposals for the future of Northern Ireland that have been canvassed by parties and analysts. We

---

* Options (a) - (d) are discussed in § 6.4 -17 and then compared with option (e), i.e. our model of shared authority.
** In important technical senses our model of shared authority implies that the relationships between Northern Ireland and the UK, and Northern Ireland and the Republic, would necessarily be federal, and potentially confederal (see paragraphs 6.23.5 and 6.24.4).
*** Options (i)-(iii) are discussed in § 6.21-25 and compared with our model of shared authority.
**** These two strategies are discussed in § 6.26-28. We argue for the superiority of (II), and that shared authority is the best way of pursuing it.

Northern Ireland is part of	(i) A Unitary State		(ii) A Federation		(iii) A Confederation	
(a) the UK	centralised integration <u>or</u> devolved integration and/or electoral integration	direct rule from London <u>or</u> direct rule + Anglo-Irish Agreement	federal UK + majority rule in Northern Ireland	federal UK + power-sharing in Northern Ireland	confederal UK + local majority rule in Northern Ireland	confederal UK local power-sharing in Northern Ireland
(b) the Republic of Ireland	centralised unitary state decentralised unitary state electoral integration	direct rule from Dublin devolution + power-sharing	federal Ireland + majority rule in Northern Ireland <u>or</u> in restored (9 county) Ireland	federal Ireland + power-sharing in Northern Ireland or in restored (9 county) Ulster	confederal Ireland + majority rule in Northern Ireland or in restored (9 county) Ulster	confederal Ireland + power-sharing in Northern Ireland or in restored (9 county) Ulster
(c) an indepe-ndent state	centralised unitary state	power-sharing + minority safeguards	Northern Ireland is cantonised, allowing local majority rule	Northern Ireland is cantonised but with localised power-sharing	Northern Ireland is fragmented into majority-rule mini-states	Northern Ireland is fragmented into power-sharing mini-states
(d) partitioned between the UK & Republic	minor repartition major repartition + population transfers	irrelevant	irrelevant	irrelevant	irrelevant	irrelevant
(e) under co-sovereignty	N/A	centralised dual direct rule from Dublin and London <u>or</u> shared authority includes peoples of Northern Ireland	N/A	[Under shared authority relations between Northern Ireland and the UK and the Republic are partly federal in character]	N/A	[Under shared authority relations between Northern Ireland and the UK and the Republic are partly confederal in character]
	(I) *Public* *Policy* *eliminates differences*	*(II)* *Public* *Policy* *manages differences*	*(I)* *Public* *Policy* *eliminates differences*	*(II)* *Public* *Policy* *manages differences*	*(I)* *Public* *Policy* *eliminates differences*	*(II)* *Public* *Policy* *manages differences*

Table 6.1.   Options for the Future of Northern Ireland.

first consider the options for statehood, then the possible forms of territorial government, and finally the possible public policy strategies a British and/or Irish government might pursue.

(a) Northern Ireland as part of the UK state

6.4. Northern Ireland could remain exclusively part of the UK as unionists insist it should, and as the British Conservative party sometimes suggests it wants. This option is the status quo, albeit qualified by the Anglo-Irish Agreement which allows the population of Northern Ireland to secede from the United Kingdom to become part of the Republic of Ireland, if a simple majority so wishes.

6.4.1. The first problem with this option is that the status quo is surely part of the problem rather than the solution. Northern Ireland is the most internally politically violent region in the European Community. The status quo is the by-product of continuous British misrule under the Union, both before and after 1920, and before and after 1972. There are, however, some who argue that the problem is not that Northern Ireland is part of the UK, but rather the way that it has been and is part of the UK. We shall examine these arguments presently (see paragraphs 6.22.2 and 6.27.3-4).

6.4.2. A second problem with this option is that it is not attractive either to the British or Irish public. In July 1991 the option of integrating Northern Ireland into the UK was the first preference of a mere 13 per cent of respondents in Britain, and of 6 per cent of respondents in the Irish Republic in the JRRT/Gallup polls.[29] Neither the British nor Irish public want Northern Ireland to be wholly integrated into the United Kingdom. In the same poll it was, however, the most-favoured first-preference of the citizens of Northern Ireland, attracting 39 per cent support (consisting of 61 per cent of Protestants but only 8 per cent of Catholics polled).[30] It is, nevertheless, abundantly clear that the British public do not regard Northern Ireland as truly or unequivocally British. Polls consistently show that the British public would prefer a UK without Northern Ireland. In the JRRT/Gallup polls the British public gave most support to options which entail relinquishing British sovereignty over Northern Ireland or sharing it with the Republic.

6.4.3. A third problem is that Irish nationalists of all hues regard the status quo as unjust, and that sense of injustice motivates both constitutional nationalism and republican paramilitaries. Nationalists argue that the Irish people were denied their right to self-determination when Ireland was partitioned during 1920-22, and unjustly and badly partitioned. They believe that the Government of Ireland Act of 1920, and the Treaty between Great Britain and the Irish Free State in 1921 were imposed by British might - Lloyd George's threat of immediate and terrible war - rather than by consensual agreement. Irish nationalists can argue under international law that the partition of Ireland was unjust (see the note accompanying paragraph 5.12); and they also have very good grounds, under the liberal theory of self-determination which we have accepted as the premise of our discussion, for believing that the pattern of partition was unjust.* Preserving the status quo does not resolve or rectify this injustice. The status quo merely suggests that the emergence of a simple majority for Irish unification - within a political structure which was expressly designed to prevent that possibility - will not be blocked by the British government.

---

*   We find the attempt of the Cadogan Group to gloss over the nature of the partition of Ireland insensitive both to fact and moral argument. Having accepted that the border 'may' have been 'unwisely drawn' they then argue that 'Wherever it was to be drawn, however, a border was inevitable, and it is perverse to portray partition as undemocratic, or morally wrong, or indeed, as doomed to failure.' They also argue that 'Ireland was partitioned in the 1920s for the same reason that Yugoslavia has been partitioned in the 1990s - there was no basis of unity'. (The Cadogan Group *Northern Limits* op.cit. (1992) p. 4 and p. 24).

We do not agree that the partition of Ireland was inevitable, or that there was no basis for unity, though it is fair to say that partition was foreshadowed in the controversies surrounding home rule. Moreover, it is not perverse to portray the particular pattern of partition as undemocratic - after all it did not respect the preferences of the majority in Ireland or of a very large minority in what became Northern Ireland. While we can agree that even the badly structured partition implemented after 1920 was not 'doomed to failure' any account of the constitutional failure of Northern Ireland which neglects the perceived injustice of its foundation simply begs the question posed by Irish nationalist critics. The comparative reference to Yugoslavia is also depressingly casual and ethnocentric. Any mildly detached observer knows that the injustices resulting from the partitions now occurring during the war of the Yugoslav succession will create a future politics of ethno-nationalist grievance in the successor states. Slovenia is likely to be the sole exception as it is (so far) the most ethnically homogeneous of the successor states.

6.4.4. A fourth difficulty is that this option supposes that the UK, and the British government in particular, can resolve the Northern Ireland conflict primarily though an internal solution - albeit allowing for good neighbourly relations with the Republic of Ireland. There is, sadly, precious little historic evidence for this point of view. The former Irish prime minister, Charles Haughey, used to argue that Northern Ireland was 'a failed political entity' in which systematic political domination and economic discrimination have been endemic since its inception. His judgement has considerable factual validity. British government, whether indirect between 1920 and 1972, or direct after 1972, has not, to date, resolved any of the major causes of conflict in Northern Ireland. The inference which we draw is a simple one: *the claim that Northern Ireland is and should be (exclusively) British is part of the problem.* Neither the British government not Ulster unionists have ever been able to persuade more than a small minority of Catholics that the UK state will treat them as full and equal citizens, and administer the region justly or impartially. Moreover, successive British governments, including Margaret Thatcher's administration, have refused to integrate Northern Ireland fully into the UK, partly because they do not believe that Northern Ireland is unequivocally British, and partly because they believe that option would so antagonise Irish nationalists that it would prove unworkable. They have recognised since 1972 that there must be an Irish dimension for the government of Northern Ireland.

6.5. Keeping Northern Ireland within the UK is defended on the grounds that it is democratic (the local majority desire it); and that it is better than the alternatives in offering the prospects of good government, security and economic prosperity. We believe, by contrast, that

• the legitimacy and democratic nature of Northern Ireland's status as part of the United Kingdom is at the very least highly questionable, for reasons already addressed in Chapter 5;

• to date no British government, acting on its own, has demonstrated that it can offer stable, widely legitimate and good government - in the form of an impartial administration of justice and public policy, and equality of treatment of the two communities within the region;

• the British government's unilateral capacity to offer effective security is highly questionable;

• the economic status quo is not sustainable in the long run because the existing levels of subvention of Northern Ireland will come under increasing administrative and political scrutiny in the absence of a political settlement in the region, especially as there appears to be a ratchet-effect in the subvention (see Figure 5.1).

6.6. Above all we do not believe that this option can successfully provide a durable resolution of the crisis of Northern Ireland - even if the constitutional parties within Northern Ireland were temporarily to agree on establishing an internal devolved government in the region (as envisaged under Article 4 of the Anglo-Irish Agreement). We do not believe that this development would be durable for two reasons:

(i) Keeping Northern Ireland exclusively part of the United Kingdom offers no prospect of terminating the IRA's activities or diminishing hard-line support for Sinn Féin. No one should wishfully pretend that this option can neutralise or eradicate militant republicanism, unless it is accompanied by extreme and wholly unacceptable repression which would endanger the free societies of Britain and the Republic. The continuation of republican paramilitary violence, and the pressures which it and the reactions to it will impose on any purely internal devolved government will significantly constrain the stability of such a government.

(ii) The second reason is just as significant. Northern Ireland is, or at least is widely perceived to be, a demographic time-bomb. The latest 1991 census returns confirm popular experience, informed journalistic and academic commentary of the last twenty years, and evidence accruing from the building and closing of schools in the region. The interpretation of the census is, naturally, a matter of some controversy. However, no informed person disputes that cultural Catholics, i.e. people born into Catholic families, who as adults are very likely to vote either for the SDLP or Sinn Féin, are now over 40 per cent of the population, or that their numbers are growing more rapidly than the community of cultural Protestants, who invariably vote for unionist parties. The demographic structure of the cultural Catholic population is distinctly younger than that of cultural Protestants. In the past the tendency of the Catholic population to grow faster than that of the Protestant population was offset by differential migration: Catholics left Northern Ireland in disproportionately higher numbers than Protestants.[31] This offsetting factor may no longer operate. Moreover it is axiomatic that the fairer the system of government and employment in Northern Ireland becomes, the more likely it is that cultural Catholics will have less reason to emigrate. In other words there is a paradox here: good and fair government in Northern Ireland is likely to result in an expanded nationalist electorate. The consequences of this demographic shift have already begun to make themselves felt in the rising share of support for nationalist parties in Northern Ireland elections since 1969. [32] In short, there is a serious prospect that within a generation a majority could develop which would favour taking advantage of Northern Ireland's present right to secede from the United Kingdom. This possibility already creates fear and insecurity amongst unionists and loyalists. They respond by demanding that Northern Ireland should be declared forever part of the Union or a non-negotiable part of the United Kingdom. We believe, however, that to accede to this request would be to provide legitimacy to the IRA and would be a complete denial of the idea that the Union should be preserved by consent. But the demographic shift and the possibly dramatic consequences which this shift might generate have to be faced. Either unionist politics and the unionist community do not adjust to it, and Northern Ireland drifts or breeds towards the eventual crisis of a 50 per cent + 1 nationalist majority without having resolved any of its core antagonisms; or, by contrast, unionist politics do adjust, in which case they will have to recognise that a political accommodation entails adjusting the nature of the Union now, and recognising the wish of most cultural Catholics to be constitutionally linked to the Republic of Ireland - in other words moving in the direction of shared authority.

6.7. We agree with the most recent Conservative Secretaries of State for Northern Ireland, Peter Brooke and Sir Patrick Mayhew, that there is no longer any strategic reason why the British government should wish to keep Northern Ireland within the United Kingdom.* However, that does not mean that British governments can lightly claim past or present 'neutrality', or that Britain has no responsibility for the present state of affairs. True, the British government is not in Northern Ireland for economic reasons (if it is the 'ruling class' must be advised by some extremely incompetent accountants). However, we should not forget that partition did keep the then most industrious and prosperous region of Ireland within the Union, and thereby impaired the economic

---

*   See the address by Peter Brooke, 'The British Presence', delivered at the Whitbread Restaurant, London, to the British Association of Canned Food Importers and Distributors (9 November 1990), and the address by Sir Patrick Mayhew, 'Culture and Identity', delivered at the Centre for the Study of Conflict, University of Ulster at Coleraine (16 December 1992). Secretary of State Mayhew has now reverted to a more traditional unionist stance, following John Major's decision to become more unionist than the unionists in the light of his party's small parliamentary majority.

development of the Republic - and the border regions of Northern Ireland. The British government did not anticipate that Northern Ireland would become an expensive liability - in fact it originally anticipated that Northern Ireland might contribute a surplus to the British Treasury - so we should not retrospectively construe Britain's commitment to the region as an act of disinterested charity. Moreover, successive British governments did have a strategic military reason for supporting the formation and maintenance of Northern Ireland - the island of Ireland used to be strategically vital for British geo-political security. That interest has now disappeared, but it would be dishonest to pretend that it was not one of the most significant reasons why British governments left the Ulster Unionist Party in control of the region until the 1960s and made no effective efforts to ensure fair administration. However, if at long last all British political parties can agree that there is no strategic interest in maintaining exclusive UK sovereignty over Northern Ireland then the question can be posed in Britain (for the first time free of self-interest): what option for the future of Northern Ireland is most likely to result in a fair, democratic, economically viable and stable region ? We submit that the status quo is just not a credible answer to such a question. *

---

* The version of the status quo which would be closest in spirit to our proposals might run along the following lines. Consistent with the spirit of the Anglo-Irish Agreement Northern Ireland remains part of the UK if the majority so wish; but if a majority of 50% + 1 support a united Ireland, sovereignty of Northern Ireland is transferred to the Republic. However, while maintaining these provisions a new British-Irish Treaty is negotiated to establish shared-responsibility institutions, which would remain in place if and when sovereignty of Northern Ireland was transferred to the Republic. These shared-responsibility institutions, which would resemble those outlined in Chapter 4, would be entrenched, possibly requiring a two-thirds majority within Northern Ireland before they could be dismantled. Such institutions might make the status quo more acceptable and would help cushion the transfer of sovereignty once there was a majority in favour of a united Ireland. They would help develop mutual trust and understanding between the two communities in Northern Ireland. The British-Irish Treaty would also set down the rights and responsibilities within Northern Ireland of the British and Irish governments. While Britain retains sovereignty the Treaty would specify the right of the Republic to represent the minority Irish nationalist community within Northern Ireland; but, reciprocally, if sovereignty was transferred to the Republic Britain would be granted the same rights and responsibilities

6.8. To summarise on this option: continued exclusive UK sovereignty over Northern Ireland is not defensible, morally or politically, and is not likely to be durable; a declaration of permanent UK sovereignty over Northern Ireland would be a violation of the Anglo-Irish Agreement, and inconsistent with any reasonable interpretation of the principle of self-determination, and the idea that the Union should be based on consent; and lastly, the status quo is likely to be characterised by continual instability and regular political violence with its attendant costs.*

(b) Northern Ireland as part of the Republic of Ireland

6.9 Northern Ireland could be incorporated into an all-Ireland state as Irish nationalist parties want, either now or in the long run. This option has considerable support in these islands, and has historically been backed by most of the British and Irish socialist and liberal left. There are 'technocratic anti-partitionist' arguments which provide some persuasive reasons why an all-Ireland polity might deliver widespread economic and political benefits for both communities in Ireland. 33 If these arguments were valid then it would follow that the national conflict, ethnic antagonisms, and political violence in a post-unification Ireland would diminish.

6.10. However, the enterprise begs so many questions; and just as exclusive British sovereignty over Northern Ireland is part of the problem rather than the solution, it may be fairly responded, by unionists and others, that *the wish to see a united Ireland, and exclusively Irish sovereignty in Ireland, is also part of the problem.*

6.10.1. There are several major difficulties with a unified Ireland. The first is that although the idea is popular in these islands it is not the option most supported in Northern Ireland. In July 1991 JRRT/Gallup polls conducted in Great Britain, the Republic of Ireland, and Northern Ireland, showed that when given a choice of options for the future of Northern Ireland a united Ireland was the most-favoured first-preference solution of the citizens of the Republic (41 per cent) and those of Great Britain (21 per cent). However, the same poll showed that it was the third most-favoured

---

to represent the minority British community within the island of Ireland.

* We address below the argument that it has been the *form* of British government in Northern Ireland that has been the problem rather than its *presence* (see paragraph 6.27 ff.).

first-preference solution in Northern Ireland - backed by just 14 per cent of respondents.* Moreover, this option did not command majority first-preference support in any of the three jurisdictions - although no other option canvassed passed this test. Even though support for Irish unity amongst Catholics is underestimated in the JRRT/Gallup polls, as in all other polls, because Catholics over-state their moderation and are afraid of being identified as subversives, the fact remains that an all-Ireland state is opposed by a majority of Northern Ireland's electorate. Therefore this option cannot be presently implemented with the consent of a majority in the region. In the JRRT/Gallup polls a whole 2 per cent of Protestants favoured the integration of Northern Ireland into the Republic as their first preference, and a further 1 per cent chose it as their second preference.

6.10.2. A second difficulty is that over nine hundred thousand Ulster Protestants (just over 55 per cent of the population of Northern Ireland) believe that they are British, at least in political citizenship, and believe that the Union of Britain and Northern Ireland should be preserved. They also believe, rightly or wrongly, that as a local majority their preferences should be 'paramount' in determining the status of Northern Ireland, and they want that status to be part of the United Kingdom. They think they would be economically impoverished, politically dominated and religiously oppressed in an all-Ireland state. They have regularly demonstrated their willingness to fight to prevent such an assimilation, in 1886, 1893, 1911-14, 1920-2, and most ferociously during 1971-6. They also vote in ways which make plain that their negative views on Irish unification are firmly, widely and sincerely held.

6.10.3. A third difficulty is that Irish nationalists have consistently failed to persuade Ulster Protestants that they are and should be part of the political Irish nation, even if many of them have thought of or do regard themselves as culturally Irish. In consequence very few Ulster Protestants regard an all-Ireland state as a desirable proposition for them. The Irish Constitution (when properly understood) supports achieving Irish unity by consent. So do all major constitutional parties in the Republic of Ireland (with the possible exception of Democratic Left, and sections of Fine Gael and the Progressive Democrats). It is also the policy of the British Labour

---

*   See the note accompanying paragraph 2.5 which explains why polls probably underestimate support for Irish nationalism in Northern Ireland.

Party. However, the arguments for unity-by-consent have not moved Ulster unionists, nor are they likely to do so in the near future. * Short of rapid demographic transformations, it is difficult to see how even a simple majority for Irish unity by consent can be quickly built in Northern Ireland, even through the concerted effort of the British and Irish governments. Unification by the consent of a bare majority of Northern Ireland's present electorate - let us say 51 per cent - would require 16 per cent of Northern Ireland's electorate which has previously supported the unionist parties to be persuaded of its merits, and would require them to vote together with *all* those who vote for northern nationalist parties in a referendum which posed the possibility of joining the Republic of Ireland. This outcome is very unlikely to occur in the next decade. Unity by consent is a long term goal; it does not provide an immediate strategy for government: Labour therefore needs a more robust policy for Northern Ireland now (to build widespread support for it), and before 1996-7 (when the next general election is due). **

6.10.4. Even if 'bare consent' - i.e. a simple mathematical majority - for Irish unification materialised before 2,003, implementing this preference without more substantial cross-community support or without the experience of shared authority institutions might provoke more severe violence than exists at present - and a unilateral declaration of independence by Ulster unionists, who might do what their predecessors did between 1911 and 1914. Even dramatic unilateral concessions by nationalists - such as a decision by the IRA to lay down its arms, by Sinn Féin, the political party which supports the IRA, to commit itself to peaceful constitutional change, and by all nationalist parties to give Northern Ireland extensive autonomy within the new all-Ireland state - might not persuade more than a tiny fraction of Protestants to consider changing their political national identity. If an organisation whose political limb obtains around 10 per

---

* The form of 'persuasion' exercised by the IRA, and other nationalist paramilitaries has been utterly counter-productive. The fact that constitutional nationalists and the IRA and Sinn Féin share the goal of Irish unification - even though they mean very different things by it - makes it more difficult for constitutional nationalists to have their arguments heard by unionists.
** The same argument holds true for the Liberal Democrats (many of whose members support Irish unity by consent) and who in our opinion are most likely to support any future Labour government engaged in a reasonable and constitutional reconstruction of the Union, in Scotland, Wales and Northern Ireland.

cent of the regional vote in Northern Ireland has been able to sustain a massive campaign of violence for over twenty years it does not take much to extrapolate the possible consequences of unionist dissatisfaction with a reunited Ireland.

6.11. An all-Ireland state cannot be accomplished by the consent of Ulster unionists in the foreseeable future. Could it be accomplished by coercion, rather than consent? Yes. In fact that is the only way in which it could be accomplished within the next decade. The British and Irish states could co-operate to coerce Northern Ireland into the Republic. The British state could accomplish 'Irish unification' by using its military prowess to co-operate with the Irish government to establish an all-Ireland state. It could also use its economic resources to 'persuade' many unionists to comply with this policy. However, there are four major problems with Irish 'unification' by coercion.

(i) It is not obvious that this coercive treatment of unionists would be ethically or politically better than the present maladies which flow from past and present coercive treatment of nationalists. It may be that all options for the future of Northern Ireland involve coercion, but in this context the way to appraise the use and merit of coercion is to ask whether it will be directed to fair outcomes for *both* unionists and nationalists. In our view it would not.

(ii) The overwhelming majority of Irish nationalists and an overwhelming majority of people in the island of Ireland vote for political parties which oppose Irish unification by coercion; so such a policy would have no democratic mandate within Ireland, however defined.

(iii) In any case it is not clear why the British and Irish governments should wish to embark upon such an enterprise. Forcing unionists into the Republic would be done against their will, and might provoke a semi-genocidal or 'ethnic cleansing' reaction against the more vulnerable nationalist population, rebellion by the local security forces (the police in the largely Protestant Royal Ulster Constabulary (RUC) and the largely Protestant local regiment of the British Army, the Royal Irish Regiment (RIR)), mass-migration within the British isles, and loyalist terrorism in Great Britain or elsewhere. No British government would wish to embark upon an enterprise fraught with so much potential danger, and the Irish government would not want it to do so. The Republic's government and electorate would not welcome managing a relatively large, recalcitrant and expensive minority forced into the Republic against its will and likely to support armed violence against the state.

(iv) Even supposing that a newly unified Ireland, created by coercion, came into being the question is could it be stable or prosperous ? The population of Great Britain is nearly 16 times that of the Republic and can presently bear the costs of the Northern Ireland subvention. In Great Britain the per capita burden of a subvention of £ (GB) 3,000 million is £ (UK) 54, whereas the per capita burden for the Republic would be £ (UK) 857. It is therefore unrealistic to expect that the Republic could at present sustain existing living standards in Northern Ireland. Moreover, uniting Ireland by coercion would mean that the causes of antagonism would have been displaced rather than remedied. The national conflict would have been 'resolved' in favour of one community at the expense of the other. Short of the Irish government building a system of control over Ulster Protestants - which might prompt them to migrate in large numbers to Britain - it is difficult to see how the new Irish state could generate stability, let alone legitimacy.

6.12. To summarise on this option: we believe that unifying Ireland through joint British and Irish coercion would be morally wrong and politically indefensible; and in any case would not work. At most territorial unification would be achieved rather than a unification of peoples. To seek the unification of the peoples on Ireland by their consent, by contrast, is a very different aspiration. While it is an aim endorsed by successive Labour Party Conferences we do not think it is a policy which can have much positive and immediate direct impact on resolving the problems of Northern Ireland.

6.12.1. We plainly do not believe in the policy of uniting Ireland by consent, and we also believe shared authority would work best if both nationalists and unionists abandoned their absolutist goals (a united Ireland and the unqualified Union). However, to those who do believe in the policy of uniting Ireland by consent we would make this argument: implementing our model of shared authority would eventually make more likely the emergence of the conditions necessary for creating, through consent, a stable and legitimate united Ireland - whether it would be unitary, federal or confederal. Our model, especially as specified in paragraph 4.20, makes it more difficult to achieve a united Ireland through a simple mathematical majority, but we have already suggested that that scenario would not result in a stable and legitimate unified Ireland (§ 6.10.4). Our model requires widespread levels of consent - above 75 per cent - before Ireland was unified; i.e. a meaningful and sustainable level of consent. However, we think that this consent would not materialise before a long and durable period of shared authority. * Yet under any plausible variation on our model it would be reasonable to expect that the co-operative experience of shared authority will make Irish unification much less threatening than it is at present.

6.12.2. We have made it plain that our model cannot, does not and should not guarantee eventual Irish unification, and it is best not advanced for that purpose. However, at least our model gives Irish unification a fair chance of being realised with broad consent, and with the experience of co-operative government. We believe that those who favour creating a united Ireland by consent should ask themselves this simple question: *if they think a model of shared authority would not work, or is not desirable, what good arguments can they offer which would show why a united Ireland would work any better?*

(c) Northern Ireland as an independent state

6.13. Loyalist paramilitaries, the former Labour prime minister, James Callaghan, and intellectuals in both parts of Ireland have canvassed the independence option for Northern Ireland. They argue for 'independence within the European Community'. They agree with us that the present conflict is primarily based on incompatible claims to sovereignty by the British and Irish states and their respective co-nationals, but instead of inviting the British and Irish governments to share sovereignty over Northern Ireland, and with its peoples, they maintain instead that the solution lies in removing both the British and Irish states from Northern Ireland. However, we believe that this option has even more difficulties attached to it than the two we have just discussed.

6.13.1. In the first place independence is strongly opposed by the vast majority of the electorate within Northern Ireland. In the JRRT/Gallup polls of July 1991 independence was far more widely supported *outside* Northern Ireland than *within* : 20 per cent of the Great British and 16 per cent of respondents in the Republic backed independence as their first-preference solution, compared with 10 per

---

* Our position is completely balanced because we would make an exactly analogous argument to those unionists who favour establishing the Union by consent: a long and successful period of shared authority would make more likely the emergence of the conditions necessary for a Union of Great Britain and Northern Ireland by consent.

cent of the electorate in Northern Ireland. These poll-results suggest widespread willingness in Britain and the Republic to be 'rid of Northern Ireland' rather than a mature belief that Northern Ireland has the material and cultural conditions necessary to forge an independent democratic state. *

6.13.2. Unionists reject independence because it would mean they would no longer be British in their citizenship, and would be bereft of the material benefits of the British connection, whereas nationalists reject independence both because they would not be part of the Irish Republic and because they would be a vulnerable minority within the newly independent state. Independence appears just because it is like splitting the difference: both sides lose their most-preferred nation-state. However, we believe that unlike shared authority the conditions for a political accommodation would not be present and could not be forged. Unionists would not be prepared to endorse widespread power-sharing or affirmative action; nationalists would not abandon their wish to see a united Ireland; and both communities would differ radically over how law and order should be administered. The two communities are very unlikely to share authority, power and responsibility under independence.

6.13.3. One advocate of independence, the Irish historian Liam de Paor, maintains that '60 per cent of the population could only oppress 40 per cent with British backing and consent' and that with external guarantees 'the unionists could not oppress the nationalists without bringing their province into chaos and ruin'. [34] We are not so sanguine. As we can see nightly on our television screens many ethno-nationalist communities in Europe and elsewhere have shown themselves more than willing to risk chaos and ruin to win perceived security. Indeed since some nationalists would see independence as a half-way house to Irish unity, the IRA would be encouraged to continue its campaign for a united Ireland after Britain had left, which would provoke predictable reactions from loyalist paramilitaries and unionist politicians.

6.13.4. British and Irish policy-makers have always rejected independence for Northern Ireland because they do not believe such a state could be stable. This fact presumably explains why Article 1 of the Anglo-Irish Agreement allows a majority in Northern Ireland to

---

*   We believe, sadly, that support or sympathy for 'troops out' amongst some sections of the English left has little to do with support for Irish nationalism, and even less for the peoples of Ireland.

determine whether the territory is to belong to the UK, or to the Republic, but it does not permit such a majority to choose independence. At present a unilateral declaration of independence is likely to materialise only in the aftermath of a precipitate British withdrawal, but in such a scenario the new state would not be founded upon principles of accommodation and therefore in our view is not worth advocating. Indeed an independent Northern Ireland created in such circumstances would almost certainly be accompanied by 'ethnic cleansing' and re-partition.

6.13.5. An independent Northern Ireland in present circumstances could rapidly become an economic basket-case. The simple withdrawal of the British subvention would lead to a precipitate fall in living standards. On the existing subvention the per capita subsidy of the Northern Ireland population is over £ (UK) 1,900 per annum.* Northern Ireland could, of course, be 'viable' as an independent state but the economic costs would be extraordinarily high, and to avoid a precipitate economic collapse it would require extensive external support. However, such external support would be forthcoming if and only if independence had the support of northern nationalists and the government of the Republic. With such support, and external (British and European) aid, an independent Northern Ireland would be just as viable as it is today - or as it would be under shared authority. However, given the deep and perfectly rational fears of nationalists about their prospects within an independent Northern Ireland they are very unlikely to offer political support to a completely independent Northern Ireland, and without this political support external economic aid is unlikely to materialise. Without external economic support, and with internal nationalist opposition, an independent Northern Ireland would rapidly degenerate into poverty stricken and strife ridden chaos. The most able and skilled members of the population would emigrate on a large scale. Large numbers of northern Catholics would seek refugee status in the Republic, and oblige the government of the Republic to intervene in the new state. The new state would rapidly develop high indebtedness - if it could find institutions willing to make it loans. To succeed, therefore, an independent Northern Ireland, requires extensive institutional backing from both the British and Irish governments, and northern nationalists, who are all, for various reasons, likely to find shared authority a more attractive and less risky option than independence. In short any

---

* The subvention is approximately £ (UK) 3, 000 million and the Northern Ireland population is 1,573, 282 people (1991 Census) so the annual per capita subvention is c. £ (UK) 1,906.84.

sensible argument for an independent Northern Ireland rapidly becomes an argument for the British and Irish governments to pay the bills without having any constitutional responsibilities for the region. In which case the question arises for the British and Irish governments: surely shared authority offers a better form of government ?

6.14. To rule out independence for the present as a viable policy-option is not to rule out giving the peoples of Northern Ireland the maximum degree of self-government compatible with mutual political accommodation. We believe that on any reasonable version of the principle of self-determination the *peoples* of Northern Ireland should have just as much right to seek independence as to seek unification with the Republic of Ireland. However, for the reasons we have already given at several junctures, we do not believe that consent for such a change should rely on a simple mathematical majority - otherwise widespread chaos and warfare would ensue. Under our model of shared authority the peoples of Northern Ireland would have the right to seek independence from Britain and the Republic on exactly the same basis as they would have the right to seek unification with the Republic or re-unification with the UK - i.e. on the basis of a weighted majority (see paragraph 4.20). On the basis of paragraph 4.20 our model is neutral on independence, Irish unification and the re-creation of the Union. It requires advocates of these options to build sufficiently widespread support for them to make them viable. *

6.15. Finally we maintain that advocates of the merits of independence should look carefully at our model of shared authority. It creates institutions which enable the level of self-government within Northern Ireland to rise dramatically - provided there is widespread consent for such changes. Our model facilitates the progressive withdrawal of British and Irish intervention in the region - providing there is widespread consent for that option. It allows no national tradition to triumph at the expense of the other, and, on the proposal outlined in paragraph 4.20, Northern Ireland would remain intact even if one community out-grew the other, politically or demographically. In other words our model allows for the maximum feasible level of autonomy for Northern Ireland, including economic autonomy, short of full independence - providing, of course, that there is widespread support for such developments. Our model is more gradualist, more

---

* Under present arrangements an independent Northern Ireland is constitutionally ruled out under the terms of the Anglo-Irish Agreement, presumably because it is considered politically unsustainable.

institutionally stable, and more economically viable than independence, and for these reasons its merits should be apparent to advocates of independence.

(d) Northern Ireland is partitioned between the United Kingdom and the Republic of Ireland

6.16. One way of resolving ethno-nationalist conflicts is to separate the antagonistic communities through partition. This option was tried in Ireland in the 1920s, although it was executed very badly. It has led some to argue that another and presumably final, partition of Ireland could be contemplated by the British and Irish governments to rectify the errors of the 1920s. In the abstract repartition might also appear to be fair because it splits the difference. The creation of a smaller, more homogeneously unionist and Protestant, British region in north-eastern Ireland, and a larger Republic of Ireland which incorporated the majority of Northern Ireland's present nationalist and Catholic community superficially might appear to rectify the errors and injustices of the 1920s. However, there are grave arguments against the merits of a second partition of Ireland, or a first partition of Northern Ireland.

6.16.1. To begin with the JRRT/Gallup polls of July 1991 showed that partition of Northern Ireland attracted a mere 1 per cent level of first-preference support within Northern Ireland. While 2 per cent of Protestants favoured it, 0 per cent of Catholics concurred. Repartition of Ireland also had low levels of first-preference support in the Republic (5 per cent) and in Great Britain (4 per cent). Not surprisingly repartition proposals are not publicly favoured by any British, Irish or Northern Irish political party. They are right not to do so.

6.16.2. Re-partition of Ireland has been canvassed only by academics prepared to think the unthinkable. In doing so they have done public policy-makers a service because they have clarified the difficulties involved. The most intelligent and constructive case for repartition has been advanced by Dr Liam Kennedy. [35] However, as Kennedy recognises, organising a just and stable re-partition would be very problematic given the distribution of the relevant populations in Northern Ireland. In three out of Kennedy's four possible partitions of Northern Ireland, west Belfast would remain in British Ulster; and his most extensive partition would still leave substantial minorities on the 'wrong' side of the new borders. None of the partitions concerned follow recognisable 'natural', cultural or political boundaries.

6.16.3. There would be major problems of consent and coercion in any major re-partition. To begin with the question would have to be asked: at which level of administration would people be given the right to exercise self-determination ? Would it be the county (now an administratively meaningless entity), the local government district, the parliamentary constituency, the electoral district or the ward ?

6.16.4. What of those who would lose out under the new arrangements ? Would they be compensated ? If so, by how much ? Would inducements have to be offered to make people move ?

6.16.5. How stable would any new partition be ? Under European Community law it is not possible to stop people residing in the territories of other member-states. Under existing British and Irish law citizens of the two states have reciprocal voting rights in the other's jurisdiction. Wouldn't the much territorially reduced British Northern Ireland be vulnerable to salami-partitions - as border-area after border-area developed nationalist-majorities ?

6.16.6. The threat of partition might induce co-operative behaviour, but it also might lead agents within Northern Ireland to engage in pre-emptive action. If one's area is a possible site for a partition the temptation will arise to 'cleanse' it of one's ethno-national opponents. This possibility is very real - and has occurred on European soil several times this century, and people already complain that it is happening in Northern Ireland (in East Tyrone, North Armagh and Fermanagh). Moreover, the numerous lives lost in previous British administered partitions of former colonial possessions (e.g. India, Palestine and Ireland) cannot inspire much confidence in the merits of any proposal that another British government could rectify the botched settlement of 1920-22.

6.17. We have argued that Northern Ireland is illegitimate because it was created and exists against the consent of a large minority of its population; but by the same token compelling the creation of a united Ireland would be just as illegitimate because it would be created without the consent of a large minority of its proposed population. The first actually illegitimate state originated in an imperfect partition. The second hypothetical state would occur because of a different mismatch between state boundaries and national communities. The re-partitionist correctly recognises the core problem at stake, but the re-partitionist solution is drastic and dangerous, and likely to produce outcomes worse than those that prevail at present. The principled re-partitionist way to resolve the 'double minority problem' is to hold locally based plebiscites in every (specially defined) part of Northern Ireland to allow people to resolve the status of their area; offer people ample and generous compensation to move from their residences and for the loss of their property, employment and their (actual and expected) welfare and pension-benefits. Given the difficulties with this way of resolving the contesting claims to self-determination in Northern Ireland, we think that the case for sharing sovereignty is strengthened. Finally, it is worth observing that we are not wishful optimists. We are prepared to think the unthinkable. We accept that a pessimistic advocate of another partition of Ireland may have grounds for doubting that it is possible to design institutions which will enable the two communities in Northern Ireland to live together peacefully, and democratically. To such sceptics we make a simple plea: surely an experiment in shared authority should be allowed to precede the more dangerous experiment of another partition ?

Comparing the big five Options on Statehood

6.18. Consider now the merits of sharing sovereignty against the other four big constitutional proposals for resolving Northern Ireland's statehood. Consider first the acceptability of the five options to the peoples with a stake in the conflict: the peoples of Northern Ireland and their co-nationals in the Republic of Ireland and Britain. Table 6.2 presents our judgements on the acceptability of the five major options in the eyes of Northern Ireland's nationalists and unionists, and the British and Irish electorates. Table 6.2. assumes that the British electorate - as opposed to particular Conservative and Labour politicians - has weakly held preferences: at the margin they would accept any solution which led to peace. That said the British electorate favours either relinquishing British sovereignty over Northern Ireland or sharing it with the Republic. Table 6.2. assumes, also consistent with polling evidence, that the Irish electorate has more strongly held preferences than the British electorate, strongly dislikes undiluted British rule in Northern Ireland, and is prepared to accept all-Ireland or the shared sovereignty options, and perhaps the independence option. Table 6.2. naturally assumes that the preferences of the two political communities which matter in Northern Ireland are very strongly held.

6.18.1. The preference-structures of the four communities can now be crudely summarised.

Is the macro-solution acceptable to

Northern Ireland's status	nationalists in Northern Ireland ?	unionists in Northern Ireland ?	the British electorate?	the Irish electorate ?
	preferences are very intense	*preferences are very intense*	*preferences weakly held*	*preferences moderately held*
part of an all-Ireland state	yes	no	very acceptable to > 33%	very acceptable to 55%
part of the UK	no	yes	no: very acceptable to 5-10%	no: very acceptable to 5%
an independent state	no	no	yes: very acceptable to 25-33%	yes: very acceptable to 35%
partitioned between Britain and Ireland	no	no	no: very acceptable to 5%	no: very acceptable to 5%
governed through shared authority	yes	no	yes: very acceptable to 25%	yes: very acceptable to 45 %

Table 6.2. The acceptability of options
Source: adapted from B. O'Leary and J. McGarry *The Politics of Antagonism* (London: Athlone, 1993).

Note: Estimates of the levels of acceptability of options are based on poll-data tapping first and second preferences (B. O'Leary, 'Public Opinion and Northern Ireland Futures' *Political Quarterly*, 1992) which is why the estimates do not add to 100.

- Irish nationalists in Northern Ireland prefer (a) a united Ireland options to (e) shared sovereignty; and they prefer shared sovereignty to (b) undiluted British rule in Northern Ireland or (c) independence or (d) a new partition. They are mostly indifferent between the latter three options, although the order in which we have presented them in reflects our judgement of their most likely preference-ranking if they were obliged to choose.

- Ulster unionists prefer (b) undiluted British rule in Northern Ireland to (c) independence; independence to (d) a new partition or (e) shared sovereignty; and any of the above to (a) any form of united Ireland.

- British voters are indifferent between (a) a united Ireland or (c) an independent Northern Ireland as their most preferred options; but prefer (e) shared sovereignty to (b) undiluted British rule in Northern Ireland or (d) a new partition.

- The Republic's voters prefer (a) united Ireland options to (e) shared sovereignty; and shared sovereignty to (c) independence, which they prefer over either (b) undiluted British rule in Northern Ireland or a (d) new partition.

6.18.2. In simple terms the four political communities preference-structures can be expressed as follows (where > means 'is preferred to', and '=' means 'is indifferent between').

Nationalists in Northern Ireland: $a > e > b = c = d$
Unionists in Northern Ireland: $b > c > d = e > a$
British public: $a = c > e > b = d$
Irish Republic's citizens: $a > e > c > b = d$.

This information about the acceptability of the five big options to the four communities enables us to reach the following conclusions:

- If each community was given an equal weight in determining the future of Northern Ireland then a united Ireland, (a), would win easily as it is the first-preference of three of them (northern nationalists, and the British and Irish publics). However, this result would not reflect differential preference-intensities across the four communities, and it is the option liked least by Ulster unionists. It is fair to rule out a united Ireland if we declare that each community should be able to veto its most unacceptable option, and this option is the most unacceptable solution for unionists.

- However, on the same decision-rule the option of undiluted British rule in Northern Ireland, (b), must be ruled out because this solution is the (or one of the) most unacceptable solution(s) to three of the four communities.

- The same reasoning also excludes a new partition, (d), because it is considered an equally bad solution by three of the four communities.

- On the premises of this argument, which weighs each of the four communities equally, the ultimate decision-choice must be between the difference-splitting solutions of independence or shared sovereignty.

6.18.3. How might this choice be resolved? It cannot easily be resolved since both Irish nationalists in Northern Ireland and the Republic prefer shared sovereignty to independence, while both Ulster unionists and the British electorate prefer independence to shared sovereignty. However, our answer, as anticipated above, is that our form of shared authority maximises the autonomy of the peoples of Northern Ireland within a framework of shared sovereignty. It splits the difference between independence and joint authority (in the form of dual direct rule). To reflect this compromise we have advocated that Northern Ireland should be given a separate international legal personality - consistent with its status as an autonomous condominium - and believe it should be enabled or encouraged to negotiate a special status within the European Community.

6.18.4. If weighting each community's preferences equally (albeit with veto-rights to rule out their worst option(s)) seems an academic and abstract way of discussing the best options for Northern Ireland consider Table 6.3. We accept that each of the five logical ways in which Northern Ireland's statehood can be resolved entail obvious and profound costs - beyond those of violating some community's preferences - and much less obvious and more intangible benefits. However, it is vital to remember that our starting point: the status quo has very considerable, persistent and predictable costs, and is unacceptable. Table 6.3. presents our worst-case judgements of the impact of each of the five big ways of resolving Northern Ireland's statehood, and shows why, on balance, the net potential benefits of shared authority exceed those of the other options on offer.

6.18.5. Our argument is *not only* that shared authority is more acceptable to more of the four communities than any other option - other than independence - when one allows each community to veto its worst options *but also* that shared authority survives our worst-case the likely impact of the big five options

Northern Ireland's status	on promoting political and legal reform and ethnic equality	on controlling political violence	on promoting political accommodation	in worst-case economic scenarios?
part of an all-Ireland state	unpredictable	poor prospects threatens more severe civil war	poor prospects	radical fall in living standards
part of the UK	poor record to date	status quo, i.e. existing civil war	status quo	sustainable
an independent state	poor prospects	poor prospects - threatens more severe civil war	poor prospects	radical fall in living standards
partitioned between Britain and Ireland	irrelevant	potentially catastrophic in the short-term, but then matters stabilise	irrelevant	sustainable
governed through shared authority	positive prospects	not much worse than status quo in the short-term but good in the medium-term	no worse than the status quo	sustainable

Table 6.3. The medium term impact of options
Source: B. O'Leary and J. McGarry *The Politics of Antagonism: Understanding Northern Ireland* (London: Athlone, 1993)

evaluations better than any of the other four options - including independence.

6.18.5.1. Shared authority is a better option than repartition because it is more acceptable to more actors - admittedly more so to Irish nationalists and the Irish government than to unionists. It is also far less likely to result in major blood-letting and ethnic cleansing than repartition. And even those who think repartition is the only long-run solution have to concede that an experiment in shared authority should precede their final solution.

6.18.5.2. Shared authority is a better option than the others in its potential for promoting the reform of Northern Ireland and controlling political violence. Compared with the status quo the presence of an Irish representative and a locally elected northern nationalist in the SACNI will give a permanent impetus for fair employment and fair administration of justice. One reason the UK state has not effectively reformed Northern Ireland is just because it is a *British* state. An Irish dimension (to match a British dimension) is indispensable to promote and implement substantive reforms which would benefit the Irish nationalist minority in Northern Ireland and ensure it genuine equal citizenship. The presence of the Irish nominee on the SACNI and the ability of the SACNI to call on Irish as well as British security forces, and a security apparatus jointly supervised by British and Irish nominees on the SACNI, will all combine to make the legitimate policing of republican paramilitary violence much easier to accomplish.

6.18.5.3. Compared with forging the political unification of Ireland our model of shared authority is much less likely to provoke an armed unionist/loyalist insurrection. The key risk of shared authority is that it is likely to lead to a short-term increase in both loyalist and republican paramilitary violence, especially the former. However, we believe that this increase in violence will prove to be short run - as the institutional protections for both communities become apparent, and British and Irish security co-operation begins to bite. Providing shared authority is not presented and defended by the British and Irish governments as a short-stay staging post to Irish unification, it will perform no worse than the other options in promoting the prospects for a long-term political accommodation, and should do better. The outraged reaction of unionists to the Anglo Irish Agreement suggests that achieving an accommodation will be difficult under shared authority.

However, we believe that:
(a) Our model of shared authority can and will eventually be seen by unionists as a distinct improvement on the Anglo-Irish Agreement because it is accompanied by three key differences:
- (i) substantive modification of Articles 2 and 3 of the Constitution of Ireland (see § 4. 19);
- (ii) dual constitutional guarantees of Northern Ireland's dual status (which gives each community a practical veto on constitutional change) by Britain and the Republic (see § 4.19-20); and
- (iii) guarantees unionists direct access, as of right, to the key political institutions in Northern Ireland - a share in the SACNI, a proportionate share in the seats of the APNI, and a share in determining the appointment of judges on the Supreme Court and ministers to administer the region.

(b) In addition, under the recommendations in paragraph 4.20, unionists will be much better protected against becoming a minority than they are at present. Under the Anglo-Irish Agreement their community can be incorporated into the Republic on a 50 per cent + 1 headcount. Our model of shared authority, unlike the Anglo-Irish Agreement, is therefore not vulnerable to the challenge that it is unbalanced or unfair.

(c) Our model of shared authority is much more boycott-proof than other options because it is not in the interests of moderate unionists or nationalists to abstain from participating in its institutions. If either bloc boycotts the political institutions then they leave their opponents in control of executive, assembly and judicial institutions; if both boycott them then the British and Irish governments in effect are left as dual direct rulers of the region.

6.19. We recognise that shared authority - especially our version of it - remains a comparatively novel idea for Northern Ireland. We also recognise that until recently it had not been widely discussed, and has attracted little public support. In the JRRT/Gallup polls of July 1991, to which we have regularly referred, respondents were asked to appraise the merits of Northern Ireland having 'a devolved government jointly guaranteed by and responsible to the British and Irish governments'. This attractively worded 'democratised condominium' option attracted the first-preference support of 19 per cent of those interviewed in the Republic, 10 per cent of those in Great Britain, and 7 per cent of those in Northern Ireland; and the second-preference support of 26 per cent of those in Great Britain, 25 per cent of those in the Republic and 11 per cent of those in Northern Ireland. These polls suggested a considerable convergence of public opinion in Britain and the Republic where respondents were far more willing to agree that both British and Irish dimensions need recognition in Northern Ireland. Citizens of Britain are very willing to give the Irish government a major role in any new settlement (49 per cent), a considerable fraction is prepared to grant a minor role to the Irish government (25 per cent), and only 11 per cent express the wish to exclude the Irish government from any new settlement. In fact more of the British public (49 per cent) think the Irish government should have a major role in the affairs of Northern Ireland than think the same should apply to their own government (32 per cent)! There will therefore be considerable British goodwill for any British government which set out to negotiate a model of shared authority with the Irish government. In the Republic there is a reciprocal widespread willingness to accept a 'British dimension' in any future settlement, with 40 per cent envisaging a minor role for the British government and 28 per cent a major role, compared with 24 per cent who see no role for the British government. We recognise that the same poll shows that a democratised condominium enjoys much greater support amongst Catholics than amongst Protestants within Northern Ireland, but we believe that with effective statecraft the two governments could improve the initial levels of active support which a system of shared authority might possess in Northern Ireland. They must seek to persuade unionists that such a system offers their best hope of long-term security.

6.20. We also recognise that critics will claim that our model of shared authority is undemocratic because it will (initially) have to be imposed against the wishes of a majority of Northern Ireland's citizens. We reply first of all that Northern Ireland, at present, is not a legitimate unit of democratic decision-making and rests on coercion. Second, we maintain that four peoples, not one, have a legitimate stake in resolving Northern Ireland - the citizens of the Republic, Britain and the two peoples of Northern Ireland. Third, we insist that any constitutional solution (apart from returning Northern Ireland to unionist majority-control) has to be imposed against the first-preferences of a majority in the region - including the status quo of British direct rule. Fourth, it is our conviction, buttressed by historical evidence, that Northern Ireland cannot be democratic and stable if its institutions are to be purely British or purely Irish. Both communities in Northern Ireland regularly democratically express their wish to be governed by either the British or the Irish states. The attraction of our model is that they will both be (partly) governed by both these states, while enjoying considerable self-government. Since the governments and electorates of both Great Britain and the Republic of Ireland have direct stakes in Northern Ireland there is also no sound democratic argument which can show why they should not create a form of shared political responsibility in which the British, Irish and Northern Irish governments and peoples participate.

What form of territorial government ?

6.21. Our argument so far might be considered superficial because 'the devil is in the detail'. Return then to the dimension of Table 6.1 which supposes that there are three territorial modes of organising democratic states: in unitary, federal, or confederal forms. In their turn such states can be more or less centralised or decentralised.

(i) Unitary formulae

6.22. A unitary state is one in which sovereign constitutional authority is not divided: it is held centrally. A unitary state can range from being centralised to being decentralised but the degree of centralisation is a function of the degree of autonomy permitted sub-central governments by the central authority.

6.22.1. The UK is a unitary state. Since 1972 Northern Ireland has been centrally governed, under direct rule from Westminster and the Northern Ireland Office (tempered after November 1985 by consultation with the Irish government). To put it mildly British rule has not been a success: it is the status quo, from which we seek an improvement.

6.22.2. Unionist integrationists maintain that if the UK government resolved that Northern Ireland was part of a unitary Union for ever then the political uncertainty that bedevils the region would end, and the IRA would be demoralised and eventually defeated. This thinking is wishful, and it mirrors the thinking of those republicans who believe that all that is necessary is for Northern Ireland to be integrated into the Republic of Ireland. A sizeable body of opinion within the largest of the two unionist parties, the Ulster Unionist Party (the UUP), favours administrative integration, treating Northern Ireland 'exactly like the rest of the UK', but it is rarely specified which sub-region of the UK they have in mind - Scotland, Wales, Yorkshire, London? The most elegant response to these arguments is that of Nicholas Scott, former Conservative Under-Secretary of State for Northern Ireland: 'Northern Ireland is different, so it must be governed differently'. [36]

6.22.3. Northern Ireland used to have a majority-rule based devolved government, the Stormont parliament, which discriminated against nationalists. The Democratic Unionist Party (DUP) contains activists who would like to see a Stormont-style regime restored. However, this prospect is rejected by all nationalists, and by the British and Irish governments who insist that any devolved government must enjoy widespread consent across both communities. This option is a non-runner for all those concerned to establish fair institutions.

6.22.4. All attempts to establish an agreed, i.e. power-sharing and parliamentary, form of devolved government within Northern Ireland have failed. This goal has been advanced by successive British governments since 1972. Unionists, so far, have not been prepared to share power in a devolved government, because they think that Northern Ireland, as part of the UK, should not have different political institutions: government, in their view, should be based on majority-rule. They have not had sufficient incentives to share power because they have preferred direct rule to power-sharing.* By contrast, constitutional nationalists, especially in the SDLP, have not been prepared to accept the idea of a devolved government within the UK unless it is accompanied by both power-sharing and an institutionalised Irish dimension.

6.22.5. The idea of an Irish unitary state, formally advocated at regular intervals by Fianna Fáil in the Republic of Ireland, does not attract unionists. Not only would they find themselves wholly within what they regard as a foreign jurisdiction but also they would have no constitutional form of territorial autonomy. Even if a unitary Irish state was accompanied by extensive devolution of authority to Northern Ireland, as suggested by Charles Haughey in his speech to the New Ireland Forum, it would have no attractions for unionists. The fact that an Irish unitary state is the explicit goal of Sinn Féin and the IRA does nothing to enhance its attractiveness to unionists.

6.22.6. A unitary independent Northern Ireland is not acceptable to northern nationalists, on political or economic grounds; and those loyalists who favour independence as a last resort clearly envisage such a state as unitary and majoritarian - even if a minority within this minority have at time talked of power-sharing or 'co-determination'.

---

* The Anglo-Irish Agreement was intended to change these incentives. It has not done so, as yet, and for one major reason - the implementation of the Agreement in practice has meant little more than direct rule with consultation with the Republic.

6.22.7. To summarise: almost all unitary formulae are unhelpful in thinking constructively about the future of Northern Ireland because they are usually part and parcel of majoritarian approaches to democracy. The exceptions, the forms of unitary structure advocated by exponents of power-sharing, fail to address the national question directly, or, by default, are seen as unionist or nationalist solutions.

(ii) Federal Formulae

6.23. In a federation sovereign authority is divided between the central and sub-central governments, and the former cannot unilaterally amend the constitution. Federalists maintain that if the boundaries between the sub-central components of a federation match those between the relevant ethnic, religious or linguistic communities, then federalism can be an effective conflict-regulating device because it makes an heterogeneous society less heterogeneous through the creation of homogeneous sub-units. However, of the seven genuine federations in long-term democracies, only three achieve this effect, i.e. Belgium, Canada and Switzerland. Of these three successes Switzerland is exceptional in its stability, something which cannot be said of Belgium or Canada, although the two latter countries have been very internally peaceful. The success of federalism in regulating national, ethnic and religious conflict in these countries has also been based upon the fact that the relevant ethnic communities are generally geographically segregated.* These conditions do not apply either in Ireland or in Northern Ireland - as Northern Ireland, without some extensive partitioning and population-exchanges, is very heterogeneous.** However, these considerations have not stopped

---

*   We do not wish to exaggerate the degree of ethnic segregation in these federations, but Quebec contains 80 per cent of Canada's Francophones, and Quebec province is itself 80 per cent Francophone. Moreover, in Belgium, the Brussels region is bi-ethnic and bi-lingual.

** The 1991 Northern Ireland Census does reveal increasing and extensive segregation within Northern Ireland, especially at the level of electoral districts. David McKittrick has demonstrated that approximately half of the population live in electoral districts that are more than 90 per cent Protestant or 90 per cent Catholic. Only 7 per cent live in districts with roughly equal numbers of both religions - and even in the districts which appear mixed the two communities are often separated by so-called 'peace lines' (*Independent on Sunday*, 21.3.1993). However, to repartition around this deepening segregation would create numerous enclaves and leave too many mini-Bosnias for comfort.

some from believing that Northern Ireland's conflicts are best resolved through federal formulae.

6.23.1. Some Irish nationalists think that the best way forward lies in the creation of an Irish federation. An Irish federation might be marginally more appealing to unionists than a unitary state. However, what would its territorial components consist of ? Would it be a two-unit federation ? Would it be based on the historic provinces of Ireland ? Would completely fresh provincial units be created ? These questions matter because unless each community has territorial protection and identity - granting it self-government in a region where it is a majority - neither community has a strong interest in a federation. An Irish federation would therefore face all the problems associated with Irish unification and additional ones created by the lack of obviously legitimate provincial units, and the necessarily dramatic disruption of the institutional fabric of the Republic which would be required. Our model of shared authority, by contrast, would create much less institutional disruption, and would involve an equal role for a British dimension in the affairs of Northern Ireland.

6.23.2. Some unionists have argued that the best way forward for Northern Ireland lies in making the United Kingdom explicitly into a federation, or, alternatively, making Northern Ireland's relationship with the rest of the UK federal in character. The former argument ties discussion of the future of Northern Ireland into the major debate about the best future constitutional direction of the UK, which we choose not to address here on the grounds that Northern Ireland has a radically different character to the rest of the UK - because of its colonial origins, dual national and ethno-religious character, and history of paramilitary violence - and therefore merits separate constitutional and analytical treatment. The UK has never formally been a federation - although some political organizations hope to move it in that direction. However, even if the UK was to become more like a federation or a confederation, say after the establishment of Scottish and Welsh devolution in the late 1990s, it is not clear what significance this transformation would have for Northern Ireland. Unionists would seek a UK federation which gave them a provincial majority; not a power-sharing province. Their preferred model of a UK federation, outlined in 1987 by the Reverend Martin Smyth, Grand Master of the Orange Lodge, and leading Ulster Unionist Party MP, completely denies Irish nationalists their aspiration for an Irish dimension, and makes it clear that unionists would seek a province which they could control without interference from a federal government in London.[37] We observe therefore that most of those who favour federalising Northern Ireland's status within the UK are in fact making a none-too-subtle case for local majority rule - a solution which would be unacceptable to northern nationalists. Our model of shared authority, by contrast, would mean that Northern Ireland had a federal relationship with the UK, but also an identical relationship with the Republic - and its form of government would not be based on simple majority rule.

6.23.3. There are some within the SDLP and other Irish nationalist parties who argue that Northern Ireland's problems can be transcended within the framework of an emergent European federation. A European federation has yet to occur, and before it does we believe that Northern Ireland needs to be constitutionally addressed. Moreover, while it is true that joint membership of the European Community has aided the development of neighbourly relations between the London and Dublin governments it is not at all obvious what impact spillovers from increasing European union will have on intra-communal relations within Northern Ireland. Issues such as dual national identity, the administration of justice, militarised policing, paramilitary violence, discrimination and the distribution of local political power are not likely to be resolved as by-products of the European single market, or the development of a single European currency. The removal of tariff barriers and increased cross-border co-operation between the Republic of Ireland and Northern Ireland, if they materialise, in our judgement will not resolve a conflict centred on national identity and ethnicity - although they may make conditions more favourable for its resolution. The border across Ireland for the time being is likely to remain one of the most heavily policed in the EC - unless there is some non-European focused resolution of 'local difficulties'. Our view is that pan-European co-operation is something desirable in its own right, not something to be favoured as a panacea for Northern Ireland. We accept, however, that no future framework for resolving Northern Ireland can occur outside the EC or the Council of Europe - which is why we have built in European provisions into our model of shared authority (including roles for the European Convention on Human Rights, the European Court of Justice, and for EC foreign ministers in conditions of emergency). These European dimensions, in our opinion, may help to underpin more direct efforts to resolve the conflict. Yet we remain convinced, for reasons advanced in our appraisal of the SDLP's model of shared authority in Chapter 7, that direct European intervention in the government of Northern Ireland is inappropriate, even if it is considered feasible.

6.23.4. The abstract possibility of an independent and federated Northern Ireland is not feasible because of the lack of obvious provincial units of government, and because the fear would always be present that such units would become the bases of secessionist movements. It is also an option without advocates.

6.23.5. Those who favour federal forms of conflict-resolution should note that our arguments for shared authority have a federal character, provided one recognises that Northern Ireland will have two 'centres'. In a federation sovereignty is shared between the federal (or central) government and the sub-federal (or provincial) units. Our proposals would have the effect of making Northern Ireland an autonomous unit within a two-unit UK federation *and* an autonomous unit within a two-unit Irish federation. The logic of these relations are reflected in the provision that Northern Ireland will be co-responsible with the two central governments for any constitutional changes in the way it is run; that Northern Ireland's constitution will not be capable of being overridden by the two central governments (notwithstanding authorised emergency powers for the two central governments); and in the representation of Northern Ireland in the British and Irish parliaments. We believe that these prospective federal relationships offer the best prospects for a stable and democratic Northern Ireland.

(iii) Confederal formulae

6.24. A confederation consists of independent states or entities joined by agreement into a union of equals. The main distinction between a confederation and a federation is that the power of the central authority is delegated in a confederation but is autonomous in a federation; or, to put matters another way, in a confederation sovereignty rests with the constituent states, whereas in a federation it is shared between the federal government and the states (or provinces). Another way of distinguishing a confederation from a federation is that the former is usually a union for specific purposes (e.g. free trade or defence), whereas a federation is all-purpose. In its current form, the European Community is mostly confederal in character. Can confederal ideas assist in resolving conflict in and over Northern Ireland ?

6.24.1. An Irish confederation would be more acceptable to unionists than a unitary Irish state or Irish federation - because Northern Ireland would be an autonomous entity in such a confederation, and because a genuine confederation is easy to secede from, and because the constituent components of a confederation enjoy greater self-government than in a federation. However, for these same reasons an Irish confederation would be opposed by Irish nationalists as unstable (threatening independence), or likely to give

Ulster Protestants too much power within Northern Ireland; and in addition it would face all the economic difficulties associated with unifying Ireland. For northern nationalists this option would be considered to be no more than a repeat of the British offer in the Anglo-Irish Treaty of 1921, allowing Northern Ireland the right to opt-out of all-Ireland institutions.

6.24.2. Similar objections can be made to the idea of a UK confederation. It too would be unacceptable to northern nationalists. They would fear that if the relationships between Great Britain and Northern Ireland became confederal, then an autonomous Northern Ireland would become a vehicle for majority rule, and, conceivably, a stepping-stone to a unilateral declaration of independence by unionists. A UK confederation would also be unacceptable to most unionists, because it would be seen as a paving-stone to a complete British institutional withdrawal, and because it would entail the removal of the redistributive welfare policies associated with a federation or unitary state.

6.24.3. The existing European confederation has not resolved conflict in Northern Ireland, and it is not obvious how it can. The arguments we advanced in paragraph 6.23.3 when discussing the possibilities implicit in a European federation apply just as much to the existing European political system.

6.24.4. To those who favour confederal mechanisms for resolving conflict we would point that our proposals have a potentially confederal character. In a confederation autonomous entities unite to share responsibility for specific functions, like external relations, or to promote a single market. Under our proposals Northern Ireland will automatically remain part of the existing European confederation. Moreover, under our proposals, provided there is widespread agreement, it will be possible for the peoples of Northern Ireland to change their relations with both the Republic and the UK, so that their relations with these states become confederal rather than federal in character. In other words they could agree among themselves, at some future juncture, that British and Irish representatives would cease to have executive responsibilities in the region.

6.25. To summarise this discussion: unitary, federal or confederal formulae based on the idea of either wholly British or Irish political systems, independence, or European union do not appear to advance the search for a solution. However, our proposals, based on shared authority, would enable Northern Ireland to have explicitly federal relations with both the British and Irish political systems, and to have confederal relations within the European union. Finally, shared authority allows for the possibility that Northern Ireland's relationships with both Britain and the Republic could become explicitly confederal rather than federal in nature. We believe that these considerations reinforce our case. Shared authority responds more sensitively than the other federal or confederal options to the analysis of the Northern Ireland problem as primarily one of clashing national identities. Moreover, unlike these options shared authority is the point towards which various forces appear to be converging:

- unionists' adamant refusal to be ruled by Dublin, and their insistence on their British citizenship;

- nationalists refusal to be ruled exclusively by London, and their insistence on symbolic as well as practical equality in Northern Ireland;

- the declining enthusiasm in the Republic for outright unification; and

- the British readiness to be detached from Northern Ireland without taking the risk of abandoning all say in how it should be governed. [38]

Which public policy strategy ?

6.26. Our arguments for sharing authority have presupposed value-commitments. We have implicitly or explicitly ruled out obnoxious and inhumane ways of resolving national, ethnic and religious conflict, such as genocide, forced mass-migration, or allowing one national, ethnic or religious group to establish control over another. On that much most people can probably agree. However, the fundamental philosophical dividing line on how to resolve Northern Ireland occurs between those, on the one hand, who believe that the objective of public policy should to eliminate national, ethnic and religious differences, and, on the other hand, those who believe that the objective of public policy should be to accommodate those differences. These are principled differences, deeply rooted in contemporary conceptions of how democracies should be organised. This division is the major one differentiating all attempts at regulating national and ethnic conflicts: the key public policy choice is between strategies which seek to eliminate differences and those which seek to manage them. [39]

(I) Eliminating Differences

6.27. Since all should agree that genocide and mass-population transfers should be ruled out as ways of resolving the problems of Northern Ireland there are only two other ways of eliminating politically relevant national, ethnic and religious differences in the region. One of these ways we have already discussed - another partition - and rejected.* The other is to promote integration (political equality through equal citizenship), with the hope in the longer run of seeing full-scale assimilation of the antagonistic communities (through extensive social interaction, shared schooling and inter-marriage). This philosophical approach is favoured by many sincere socialists, liberals and conservatives. However, we believe that this approach, while mostly high-minded and sincere, in fact contributes to sustaining the conflict in and over Northern Ireland. We believe that integration is a principled, valuable and effective strategy for immigrants, who by definition are willing to trade some of their previous cultural identity for citizenship of their new state; but integration is much less likely to be a successful strategy for dealing with peoples living in their 'historic homelands', who see no reason why they should be encouraged or obliged to integrate into another community's culture.

6.27.1. Many political activists, including some conservatives, liberals and socialists, believe that the goal of public policy in Northern Ireland should be to reduce the politically relevant differences between nationalists and unionists (or between Catholics and Protestants) through civic integration. They also usually hope that successful civic integration will enable ethnic assimilation, in the form of extensive inter-marriage across the ethnic boundary, to take place later. The advocates of integrated education, and integrated housing policies share the supposition that the promotion of integration will accomplish eventual assimilation, and that such assimilation is intrinsically desirable. Most of the members of the Alliance party, predominantly composed of liberal middle class Protestants and Catholics, share these beliefs. So do some left-wing socialists and some 'one nation' conservatives. The key problem with

---

* Internal partition - in the form of 'cantonisation' - is possible. It would require an extensive re-drawing of existing local government boundaries so that units of government corresponded with 'communities on the ground'. It is similar to internally federalising Northern Ireland. However, to embark upon this strategy is tantamount to encouraging people to take steps which would lead to a repartition and 'ethnic cleansing'.

this approach, however, is that it is not neutral. It is unclear whether its exponents think public policy should be directed towards the dissolution of both ethno-national identities, whether they be defined as Protestant and Catholic, or unionist and nationalist; or whether they are in fact, if not always in explicit intention, advocating the creation of one weaker form of the political and cultural identities on offer - a semi-secularised middle class British identity in the case of the Alliance party.

6.27.2. There are two important questions to ask about civic 'integrationism': is it feasible, and is it just ? Most people recognise that compulsory ethno-religious educational and housing integration can produce considerable opposition, including violent opposition. At present using fiscal incentives to encourage educational integration in Northern Ireland would have to work at the expense of the voluntary sector in schools - i.e. the predominantly Catholic sector. However, such a policy would signal a clear message that integration is taking place at the expense of one identity rather than both. As one British Labour minister taxed with the task of investigating integrated education in Northern Ireland in 1974-5 put it: 'I became persuaded that integrated education meant Protestant education.' [40] Moreover, at present, there are no sensible or equitable ways in which a British government can force people from the two communities to live together in the same streets, council flats or housing estates. However, in the absence of coercive integration voluntary integration is all that is possible, and we know, despite the best efforts of those involved in community relations and encounter groups, that the two principal communities have become and are becoming more residentially and culturally segregated than they were before the 1960s. In short, voluntary integration is only likely to work successfully as when the major questions of war and peace, and the status of Northern Ireland, have been satisfactorily resolved.

6.27.3. The problem, as we see it, is that too many parties to the conflict are presently integrationists, but on their terms. Unionists wish to integrate Northern Ireland into the UK, administratively, electorally or culturally. In so doing they ignore or diminish the importance of their minority's Irish national identity. Irish nationalists, north and south, have and do seek the integration of Northern Ireland into all-Ireland state. In so doing they ignore or diminish the importance of the British and religious identity of 'their minority', Ulster unionists. Each community has an 'integration project'; each is majoritarian, at the expense of its own minority. National integrationists, however, are not the only integrationists. There are other integrationists, who do not recognise that is what they are. There are, for example, secular integrationists, who believe that the problem is that Northern Ireland's communities are too religious. Some (usually Protestant-born) socialists, liberals and conservatives maintain that integration into the UK party-system will advance a secular socialist, liberal or conservative agenda in Northern Ireland, whereas some (usually originally Catholic) socialists, liberals and conservatives maintain that the integration of Northern Ireland into the Republic will advance the causes of social democracy, liberalism, or conservative secularism in all of Ireland. There are also ecumenical integrationists, who believe that pan-Christian unity offers the best hope of reconciliation. In our view, all such integrationists, be they national, Christian, conservative, liberal or socialist, are engaged in varying degrees of wishful thinking. Creating civic homogeneity out of intense national, ethnic and religious divisions may seem desirable, although that is debatable, but it is hardly practical. It can only be practical if 'one side loses' - which is not immediately likely given the present stalemate - or, if there has been a preceding accommodation of differences.

6.27.4. Presently the most persistent advocates of integration as a way of resolving Northern Ireland usually deny that they are integrationists. Strictly speaking, however, they are 'electoral integrationists'. They think the problem with British government in Northern Ireland has been its form not its presence. They maintain that if 'real' British political parties, viz. the Conservatives, Labour and the Liberal Democrats, organised and competed in elections in Northern Ireland then its national, ethnic and religious politics would be transformed, and 'normal' liberal democratic politics could develop.* This argument may be high minded, but we believe it is utopian. There is first of all the fact of the historical record: electoral integration has not worked in the past. British political parties have competed in Ireland before, between the 1880s and the 1920s. Given that the UUP was affiliated with the Conservatives, and that the Northern Ireland Labour Party supported the British Labour Party, it is at least arguable that British political parties competed in Northern Ireland between the 1920s and the 1960s. Electoral integrationists questionably assume that the major cause of conflict in Northern Ireland since 1920 has been the absence of British party competition

---

* The most eloquent versions of these arguments are put forward both by liberal conservatives like Arthur Aughey (*Under Siege* (London: Hurst, 1989)) and by socialists like Hugh Roberts ('Sound Stupidity: The British Party System and the Northern Ireland Question' *Government and Opposition,* 22, 3: 313-35).

in the region, rather than the national/ethnic question.* Secondly, electoral integrationists presuppose that parties matter more than comparative evidence suggests in determining the nature of political conflicts based on nationality and ethnicity. In Europe Spanish parties organise in the Basque country without preventing conflict there, and in Belgium the three main parties have organised across the linguistic divide, but that has not stopped ethnic tensions rising between Flemings and Walloons from the 1960s. Elsewhere state-wide party organization and competition have not prevented the development of powerful local ethno-secessionist parties in democracies as large and as diverse as India and Canada. Electoral integrationists argue that Northern Irish residents will vote for British political parties in large numbers if given the opportunity, but the evidence is unpersuasive. The Conservatives, the solitary British political party to have organised in the region, lost their deposit in the European parliamentary election of May 1989, and have performed well in only one very unrepresentative local-government district, North Down. In the 1992 Westminster election the Conservatives won a mere 5.7 per cent of all votes cast in the region. Organizations seeking to persuade Labour to organise in the region have received derisory votes - which is one reason Labour refuses to do so.*

6.27.5. Electoral integrationism does not offer a promising path out of the present impasse. In the first place it would be *British* electoral integration which is being tacitly or explicitly advocated. Our counter-argument can be expressed in a generalisation: in any liberal democracy where at the outset of the system political parties originally and successfully organised across ethnic or religious lines it has helped in the democratic regulation of communal conflict; and it is usually easy to go from such a system to one where party alignments directly reflect communal cleavages; but it is extremely difficult, if not impossible, to move in the reverse direction and

---

* Hugh Roberts even claims that the British party 'boycott' of the region is '*the fundamental reason* for the continuing conflict' in Northern Ireland (see footnote above).
* See Kevin McNamara, Roger Stott and Bill O'Brien *Oranges or Lemons ? Should Labour Organise in Northern Ireland ?* (London: 1993). The authors argue that it is wrong to assume that Northern Irish voters who might, hypothetically, vote for British political parties would do so for non-national and non-religious reasons. Polling evidence confirms that the Conservatives appeal to those in favour of the Union, i.e. Protestants; whereas the Labour Party appeals to those in favour of Irish unity, i.e. Catholics.

engineer cross-national, cross-ethnic or cross-religious organization when nationalist, ethnic or sectarian parties already exist (as in Northern Ireland). Such engineering will be even more difficult where the fundamental cleavage is national or ethnic as opposed to religious.

6.27.6. We believe our model of shared authority would work best if British and Irish political parties did not organise and compete in Northern Ireland as they do in their core states. At present the Conservatives and Sinn Féin are the only significant parties which attempt to organise and compete in two jurisdictions - and in both cases they are only significantly successful in one jurisdiction. Of course, in a liberal democracy political parties must be free to organise and compete in elections as they see fit - and that is well and good, and we certainly would not want to see a constitutional prohibition on British or Irish parties organising in the region. Political parties must be free to organise if they wish to do so - that is a fundamental democratic tent. It is not, however, a fundamental tenet that they be required to organise everywhere they can. We believe that there would be little benefit for the electorate in Northern Ireland in having the four major parties from the Republic and the three major British political parties competing with the five major local parties. We believe our model would work best if local parties were the primary competitors and co-operators in Northern Ireland's political institutions, in part because they will be more responsive to local needs and interests. Naturally local parties must be free to negotiate alliances, affiliations and deals with other political parties in the Westminster, Leinster House, and European parliaments, but we believe their local predominance would help stabilise our model of shared authority.

6.27.7. Integrationism, whether it be administrative, cultural, constitutional or electoral, is mostly a symptom of conflict in and over Northern Ireland, rather than a solvent. Integrationism is mostly British or Irish, Protestant or Catholic, unionist or nationalist, and is always decoded in these ways, even if sincere exponents of particular forms of integrationism do not intend to be, or to be seen to be, aligned with one bloc or another. To sincere advocates of integrationism, who wish to transcend 'orange and green', we would make the following appeal: surely a model of shared authority, which successfully accommodated national and religious differences, and which left full civic freedom to the non-aligned and non-religious to compete for political space and influence, offers a more secure prospect that their core values will be heard and better expressed, publicly and institutionally ?

(ii) Accommodating Differences: national, religious and civic pluralism

6.28. The alternative public policy strategy to seeking to eliminate differences is to pursue a policy of accommodating differences - i.e. to aim to secure the rights, identities, freedoms and opportunities of both national-ethnic communities. This is the philosophy which has motivated our argument. It is not, to preempt misunderstanding, an argument which supposes that there are only two communities in Northern Ireland, and there are no other forms of conflict or politics. However, our philosophy does require the creation of political and legal institutions which enable both communities to enjoy the benefits of equality without forced assimilation. It requires institutionalising equal respect for both national traditions and their cultural and religious heritages, and it requires full civic and political freedom for those who do not wish to be part of the major national and religious communities.

6.28.1. The public policy of shared authority precludes any efforts by governments to force or strongly encourage people to be schooled or housed together. However, it does require full equality of public provision in public services for each community. For this reason we welcome the fact that British public policy in Northern Ireland has at last ensured that all schools - integrated, state and Catholic - are in future to receive equal levels of public funding. We regard this as a model of good consociational practice: full multi-cultural equality, including equality for those who wish to be non-aligned

6.28.2. The pluralist philosophy which motivates our argument implies a commitment to proportionality and equality in political, legal and economic work-organizations, since here national, ethnic and religious differences are likely to produce violence, instability and perpetuation of conflict. This pluralism requires bills of rights, effective fair employment legislation, institutional respect for the two major traditions; proportionality in policing and judging, and proportionality of another kind in military pacification; and mutual collective vetoes and rights on matters of collective, religious, linguistic and national autonomy. In other words it requires the elements built into our model of shared authority, outlined in Chapter 4. Democratic ethnic and civic pluralism, we believe, is best advanced through a form of shared authority that maximises the self-government and autonomy of the communities of Northern Ireland. It is also compatible with ensuring that secular, bi-confessional or non-Christian individuals, and people who are neither British nor Irish in their national or ethnic origins, can enjoy the full benefits of a democratic civil society. *

---

*   Some supporters of the Alliance party and Democratic Left may express the fear that we are proposing a communal or groups-only democracy. We assure them that this fear is misplaced. Our model entrenches individual rights and freedoms, and anti-discrimination provisions to protect individuals and non-conformists, and we have only sought to protect reasonable collective rights, and with the proviso that the equivalent rights of others are respected. In our model there is one common electoral roll for Northern Ireland, and the directly elected political offices in the SACNI and the APNI are open to competition from non-aligned individualists, or those who favour different forms of collectivism. Throughout we have consistently sought to reconcile liberal democratic principles with the fact that there is not one common cultural identity in Northern Ireland.

CHAPTER 7   MODELS OF CO-SOVEREIGNTY

7.1. Our thinking on shared authority has not emerged from the blue, nor is our model the first piece of extended reflection on the merits of sharing sovereignty. However, our model is a distinctive synthesis. It differs from transitional models of joint sovereignty discussed below because it is intended to provide a durable settlement. It differs from the models suggested by the New Ireland Forum because it is more democratic in character, richer in institutional detail and clear about the constitutional status of Northern Ireland. It differs from the Kilbrandon model of co-operative devolution because it specifies that the British and Irish governments are co-equals, and because it spells out an explicit system which separates powers and provides checks and balances within the region. Finally, it differs from the SDLP's 'commissioner model' (i) in excluding a co-equal role for a European representative, (ii) in clarifying Northern Ireland's status, and (iii) in providing for fully democratic and locally accountable structures of government.

Transitional Models of Joint Sovereignty

7.2. We know of three similar proposals which have envisaged joint sovereignty as transitional - i.e. as mechanisms for facilitating the more or less rapid establishment of Irish unification. They were made by Desmond Fennell, a nationalist intellectual in 1971[41], by the SDLP in a policy proposal in 1972 [42], and much later suggested by Michael Farrell, a lawyer and a former civil rights activist, in a submission to the Opsahl Commission of Inquiry in 1993 [43]. None of these proposals provide much institutional detail. They suffer from several faults. The major one is that while they tacitly recognise unionist opposition to a united Ireland, by implication they believe that such opposition has no moral, political or constitutional standing equivalent to that of nationalist opposition to Northern Ireland. In other words all these models are reducible to variations on promoting Irish unification without consent. We re-iterate that our conception of shared authority is not of this nature. While our model does not preclude Irish unification - should widespread consent emerge for it - it is neither conceived of as, nor is it capable of becoming, a mechanism for imposing the unification of Ireland without consent. Our model is genuinely neutral on the long-run future of Northern Ireland.

The New Ireland Forum Model(s)

7.3. The New Ireland Forum articulated a conception of 'joint authority' as the third-preference of the nationalist parties of Ireland. It implied a permanent system of dual direct rule - with British and Irish commissioners governing Northern Ireland. The Forum sub-committee envisaged two variations: (a) a vaguely specified two person Joint Authority Commission (JAC), one British and one Irish, in effect a dual ministerial prefecture, in which the commissioners could appoint deputy commissioners; and (b) an alternative model in which the JAC supervised a local executive supported by a locally elected assembly. Both variations clearly involved full co-sovereignty for the two states - although the expression 'joint authority' was used by the Irish parties so as not to intrude upon the sensibilities of the then Conservative government.

7.3.1. Under variant (a), dual direct rule, each governmental function would either be jointly exercised or an agreed division of functions within a framework of collective responsibility would operate. Each commissioner would be appointed by the respective prime minister. It is difficult to understand how law-making was conceived of in this variant - presumably necessary legislation in the respective states would be made by decree of the JAC, ratified by Orders in Council on the British side and Governmental/Ministerial Orders of the Oireachtas on the Irish side.

7.3.2. Under variant (b) the JAC would delegate functions to a devolved government (an assembly which chose its executive). Presumably, though it was not specified, it was envisaged that Northern Ireland would develop an autonomous legal personality. The Forum sub-committee report did not elaborate but the presumption must have been that the JAC could veto decisions or legislation of the devolved government.

7.4. The New Ireland Forum model of joint authority is vague, and not very rich in institutional detail. The status of Northern Ireland is not clarified - with respect to Irish constitutional law or for the purposes of international relations. In both variants of the Forum model, (a) and (b), sovereignty is vested exclusively with the two states, whereas in our model it is also shared with the peoples of Northern Ireland - who have constitutional safeguards to protect them against any proposed constitutional changes affecting the region. The absence of any local share in sovereignty for the peoples of Northern Ireland not only makes the Forum model of joint authority quasi-colonial in character, it also means that it lacks mechanisms for resolving differences between the British and Irish commissioners. By contrast our model lacks colonial traits, and has several mechanisms for resolving differences. First, the SACNI itself can operate according to majority rule principles in certain issue-domains. Second, the SACNI contains a majority of members elected by the peoples of Northern Ireland. Third, the British and Irish nominees only possess full co-sovereignty in conditions of emergency - either conditions involving local emergencies or those involving a boycott of the SACNI by all the local representatives. Third, in the security-domain we have proposed a co-operative model of operations and distinct responsibilities for the British and Irish nominees on the SACNI. Finally, in emergency circumstances where the British and Irish nominees to the SACNI cannot agree we have proposed a role for binding arbitration by a committee of European foreign ministers (excluding the British and Irish foreign ministers) who presently (i) hold the European presidency, (ii) have just held the presidency, and (iii) will next hold the presidency.

The Kilbrandon Model of Co-operative Devolution

7.5. The Kilbrandon Committee of British-based commentators, developing an initiative of their own in the absence of a detailed official and public British response to the New Ireland Forum, developed a critical and imaginative response to the deficiencies in the Forum model of joint authority. * The key ideas of the majority on the Committee were as follows:

7.5.1. They saw the need for a functioning executive which would be representative and boycott-proof. They therefore proposed a five person executive, consisting of the Secretary of State for Northern Ireland (or his/her deputy), the Irish Minister for Foreign Affairs (or his/her deputy) and three members elected by the population of Northern Ireland. This idea is the source of our own proposed SACNI. It is both representative, and makes a boycott by local representatives self-defeating, and provides for a functioning system of joint direct rule if all local representatives boycott the SACNI.

---

* The Kilbrandon Committee, an independent British response to the New Ireland Forum, made its argument in a document published under the title *Report of an Independent Inquiry 'To Consider the Report of the New Ireland Forum, Examine the Practicality of any Proposals Made in the Report by Any Other Sources, and Make Recommendations'* (London, 1984).

7.5.2. They proposed that within the executive *all* decisions be made by majority-rule. They thought that the structure of the executive would normally produce two unionists who together with a British representative would normally be decisive. The pivotal nature of the British vote in their view would reflect British sovereignty, funding and security-commitments.

7.5.3. They discussed the possibility of a legislature composed of 17 Northern Ireland members (the present level of representation of Northern Ireland at Westminster), 8 members of Dáil Éireann and 8 British Westminster MPs. The Westminster and Leinster House members would be chosen on select committee lines.

7.5.4. They wanted to involve the Irish government in law enforcement in Northern Ireland. They envisaged the Police Authority being replaced by a co-operative Security Authority (one Minister from the Northern Ireland Office, one from the Irish Department of Foreign Affairs and three members from Northern Ireland, drawn from both sides of the community). However, the Kilbrandon Committee made it clear that the Security Authority would be subject to the Secretary of State for Northern Ireland, and the British Army and the RUC were clearly envisaged as being the sole agents operationally responsible for security and law enforcement.

7.5.5. They proposed mixed courts, recommending two judge courts - one judge to be from the Republic of Ireland if the defendant so wished.

7.6. The Kilbrandon model marked a genuine intellectual watershed in creative thinking, but it nevertheless has a number of defects:

7.6.1. It does not dilute British sovereignty sufficiently to put the Irish state and Irish nationalists on an equal footing with the British state and unionists. These traits are evident in the proposals affecting security, and leaving all matters to be resolved by majority rule within the proposed Executive. The failure to ensure unanimity or constitutional equality on matters affecting national or religious rights and freedoms is a basic defect. The Kilbrandon model also gives the Republic responsibility without power or economic obligations.

7.6.2. The law-making, financial and economic policy-making mechanisms are not elaborated or clear in the Kilbrandon Committee report.

7.6.3. The proposed hybrid legislature for Northern Ireland, with an unreformed franchise for Westminster, would leave Ulster Unionists over-represented amongst the 17 Northern Irish members; and would have representatives elected under two different electoral systems (STV in the Republic and plurality-rule in the UK). In brief there is no consistent application of the principle of proportionality.

7.7.4. While the Kilbrandon Committee envisaged Northern Ireland's status being clarified along the lines of Article 1 of the Anglo-Irish Agreement - and recognised through modification of Articles 2 and 3 of the Irish Constitution - it did not in our judgement reflect sufficiently on how to define Northern Ireland's status satisfactorily, or on how to create a durable system of government with elements of shared sovereignty. By contrast, our model clarifies Northern Ireland's *new* status under shared authority, and makes it more difficult to change that status than it is to change Northern Ireland's status under the Anglo-Irish Agreement.

The SDLP's Commissioner Model

7.7. In its submission to the 1992 inter-party talks the SDLP proposed a form of government for Northern Ireland partially modelled on the European Commission - with three commissioners to be elected from Northern Ireland, and three to be appointed by the British and Irish governments and the European Community. This proposal, like that of the Kilbrandon committee, was imaginative but is inadequate in key respects.

7.8. The most visible defects of the SDLP's proposals are that:

7.8.1. The European Commission is an inappropriate model for the direct democratic government of a region - especially as the SDLP's model lacks an adequate elaboration of other necessary elements of democracy (such as a popular assembly to check and balance the executive, and a supreme court).

7.8.2. The proposed European commissioner is unnecessary, difficult to hold to account, difficult to establish - and probably difficult to find. Citizens of the European Union already complain that commissioners are unaccountable but very powerful bureaucrats, and many proposals for the reform of the European Union envisage the termination of commissioners. In any case the member-states of the European Union are not likely to welcome the prospect of commissioners directly governing regions of member-states. The present President of the Commission Jacques Delors has already publicly expressed the view that European involvement in Northern Ireland should be moral, political and economic, rather than overtly institutional.

7.8.3. In the SDLP's model it is not clear whether decision-making amongst the commissioners is meant to proceed by unanimity, or by majority rule.

7.8.4. There is a sound democratic case for the Northern Ireland executive having a majority of its members elected by the peoples of Northern Ireland - as is the case with our proposed SACNI, but is not the case with the SDLP's commissioner model. The majority of the SACNI's members should be elected by the inhabitants of the region: otherwise the colonial criticisms of condominial structures would have some force. We believe that our model has none of the difficulties we have identified with the SDLP's commissioner model.

Summary

7.9. These alternative models of co-sovereignty, whatever their defects, have helped inspire the model which we have articulated in Chapter 4, and defended in depth in Chapters 5 and 6. We hope we have made clear how and why our own synthesis is distinct from those of previous proposals. Our efforts have been directed towards designing an institutionally credible and democratic system of shared authority. Critics are welcome to improve on our proposals just as we have attempted to improve on our predecessors.

CHAPTER 8   UTOPIANISM AND REALPOLITIK

'what we call necessary institutions are often no more than institutions to which we have grown accustomed... in matters of social constitution the field of possibilities is much more extensive than people ... are ready to imagine.'
Alexis de Tocqueville, *Recollections.*

8.1. We accept that at first glance our arguments are likely to be disagreeable to both nationalist and unionist militants. Nevertheless we have tried to persuade them that our proposals offer a fair resolution of their differences, and institutional means of living together without abandoning their core values. We have put forward our proposals for public debate and criticism, and are more than willing to believe that there are ways in which they might be refined and improved upon. In due course we shall respond constructively to such criticisms as our proposals may receive.

8.2. We also anticipate that our argument will be attacked by those who are not nationalist or unionist partisans. Again we are more than willing to listen and respond to such criticisms since nobody can reasonably claim a monopoly of wisdom on Northern Ireland. From our experience of discussing these matters with friends and colleagues we anticipate two lines of criticism from those who are neither nationalists nor unionists. On the one hand our proposals might be accused of being utopian, naive and wishful, and on the other hand, they might be attacked as an exercise in cynical realism.

8.3. We accept that our proposals will be attacked by those who think it is utopian, wishful and naive to believe that sovereignty is divisible, and who think that each nation must have one state, and that each state must have only one nation. We would reply that we have argued at various junctures that it is exactly these allegedly realistic beliefs which block political progress in Northern Ireland. In particular we maintain that the belief that sovereignty must be indivisible, and that indivisible sovereignty is a 'necessary institution', is merely an idea to which we have become accustomed, indeed too accustomed in both Britain and Ireland. Our proposals, based on careful attention to constitutional, party-political and economic evidence, demonstrate that the 'field of possibilities' for Northern Ireland is much more extensive than those who parade themselves as hard-headed realists would suggest. We are happy to accept the charge of being imaginative, but we insist that our imagination has been disciplined by reality and a concern for people's expressed definitions of their interests and values.

8.4. Indeed we would accept that our argument is an essay in what German historians call *Realpolitik*: scrupulous attention to what is possible, a careful estimation of what those who are likely to disagree with us really want, and a preparedness to justify the authoritative use of governmental resources as and when that may be necessary. However, we are not cynical realists. *Realpolitik* is not the same as cynical realism: the view that 'values, ideals and law' can and should have no place in a world of pure power politics. We do not share this base and baseless view of the world: if we did there would be little point in making this argument. We are realists only in the common-sense meaning of the term: we claim to see things as they really are in Northern Ireland. We think that the core of the conflict is centred on competing nationalisms, and sharp durable ethnic divisions marked by a religious boundary. We think that any constructive resolution must address this epicentre of conflict. Moreover, it must respect the values and ideals held by each community, and by both communities, and establish a framework of constitutionality and legality appropriate to an advanced democracy. Our model does so.

8.5. Common-sense realism recognises that no party to the conflict in Northern Ireland can obtain all that it says it wants through force, or through negotiation, or through some combination of coercion and persuasion. However, that does not mean that most of the peoples of Northern Ireland cannot obtain what they really want: certainty, security for their national identity, constitutional security, legitimate government, the rule of law, and civic equality. Common-sense realism recognises that Northern Ireland has no settled constitutional or legal order: its sovereignty is disputed, its legality and legitimacy are contested, its peoples do not govern themselves, and, for different reasons, they think of the status quo as profoundly unjust and unsettling. Our proposals recognise these facts, but they also seek to change them.

8.6. Our proposals would establish Northern Ireland's constitutional status as part of both the British and Irish nations and states, and regularise and legalise that position in British public law and in the Irish Constitution. They would reduce uncertainty. They would provide self-government for the peoples of Northern Ireland, and enable them, through collective agreement, to extend that self-government as they see fit; construct security and political arrangements which would enhance both peoples' confidence in the legitimacy of governmental and legal institutions; and enable the British and Irish governments to develop their existing co-operation in a constitutionally regulated, accountable, and economically feasible manner. We believe that the British and Irish governments would win the support of the vast majority of their citizens if they negotiated an agreement along the lines of our model of shared authority, and, in so doing, would eventually bring peace to the nations of these islands.

APPENDICES

A Sovereignty, joint authority & shared authority

A.1. We have deliberately used the expression 'shared authority' rather than 'joint authority' or 'joint sovereignty'. On the one hand the term joint authority has become associated with the idea of dual direct rule advocated in the New Ireland *Forum Report* of 1984 (see Chapter 7), suggesting that the British and Irish governments directly govern Northern Ireland together, in the way, for instance, that the British and French governments ran the New Hebrides. We have called the system proposed here shared authority to emphasise that it involves a full share in democratic and accountable government for the peoples of Northern Ireland as well as the British and Irish governments.

A.2. On the other hand some political theorists, in our view wrongly, believe that sovereignty is indivisible and cannot be shared. To avoid tedious argument we have therefore used the word authority rather than sovereignty throughout - but we will not object if we are read as advocating shared sovereignty. For those who are very concerned with the definition of sovereignty we give our understanding of its relationship to our proposals below.

A.2.1. Sovereignty was a concept developed in early modern political and legal theory, especially in the writings of Jean Bodin, Thomas Hobbes, Jean Jacques Rousseau and John Austin. The first two of these authors were, significantly enough, defenders of absolutist government. Rousseau, by contrast, was the first famous exponent of popular sovereignty, while Austin was the author of the idea that valid law is the command of the sovereign. The meanings and significance of sovereignty have always been the subject of much rhetorical and symbolic dispute, and are likely to remain so whatever we might wish.

A.2.2. Sovereignty is standardly considered to be possessed by the supreme source of authority within a political system: it can therefore be vested in a person (a sovereign monarch), a parliament (a sovereign parliament), a people (a sovereign people), or a constitution (a sovereign constitution). So construed, in our proposals sovereignty is vested in our proposed constitution for Northern Ireland which specifies how valid laws may be made for the region.

A.2.3. However, sovereignty is also usually considered to possess both external and internal dimensions.
- Externally a sovereign state is formally recognised by others as possessing full authority over a given territory and its population. So construed under our proposals Northern Ireland will not be a sovereign state. Until such time as its peoples decide otherwise its external sovereignty will be vested in the internationally recognised states of the United Kingdom and the Republic of Ireland.

- Within a state internal sovereignty is possessed by that constitution, person, organisation, or body of people who have ultimate authority. So construed in our proposals the internal sovereignty of Northern Ireland will be vested in its constitution, which will be guaranteed by the Republic of Ireland and the United Kingdom.

A.2.4. Under our proposals it might also be said that *de jure* sovereignty is vested in the constitution of Northern Ireland while *de facto* sovereignty is shared by the peoples of Northern Ireland and the governments of the Republic of Ireland and the United Kingdom (who shall appoint two members of the SACNI, and possess emergency powers under the proposed constitution).

A.2.5. Four major intellectual debates have surrounded the interpretation of sovereignty. As this appendix is not an treatise in political theory we quickly elaborate below on how these debates are pertinent for our proposals.

(i) The first debate is over whether sovereignty is divisible. Some maintain that sovereignty is indivisible, pointing that the concept originated in the claims made on behalf of jurists who favoured absolutist and law-monopolising monarchs. Others have argued that the separation of executive, legislative and judicial powers in written constitutions divides sovereignty vertically, whereas the autonomous powers of federal and provincial governments within a federal political system divide sovereignty horizontally. In our proposals we believe that the constitution of Northern Ireland will vertically divide judicial from executive and legislative powers, and that Northern Ireland's relationships with both the Republic of Ireland and the United Kingdom will be federal.

(ii) There is a very similar debate over whether or not sovereignty can be pooled or shared. Traditionalists maintain that sovereignty implies monopolistic possession and therefore it cannot be shared: for them treaties are exercises of sovereignty, not allocations of shares in sovereignty. Others suggest that the evidence of federal systems and political systems which separate powers and functions establishes that there are political organs which must share responsibility and authority (as well as dividing it): and so it follows that they must share sovereignty (for them treaties are allocations of shares and duties in pooled sovereignty). Their critics maintain that in federal systems it is the constitution which is the sovereign, to which the reply is made that such constitutions specify how sovereignty is to be divided and shared; to which the reply is then made that any legal system must be unified and cannot be parcelled out amongst various bodies, and so on *ad infinitum*. The best resolution of these arguments is that of Preston King who argues that the hallmark of sovereignty is not indivisibility but rather the finality of authoritative decision. As he writes in the *Blackwell Encyclopaedia of Political Thought* 'Sovereignty can clearly be divided among a plurality of agents ... without in any way detracting from finality of decision'. [44] Our proposals would establish a plurality of agents amongst whom the sovereignty of Northern Ireland is divided (and shared), but they would also ensure 'finality of decision' for Northern Ireland, i.e. a valid and unified source of authoritative law. Naturally, to avoid misunderstanding, such 'finality of decision' does not mean that such laws cannot be challenged in the courts.

(iii) Third, following Austin, some argue that law is the command of the sovereign and that the sovereign is not subject to legal challenge. Others maintain that this viewpoint confuses legal and political sovereignty: the legal sovereign is that which authorises valid law, while the political sovereign is that which has the ability to make valid law. Under our proposals the Constitution of Northern Ireland is the authoritative source of law, but it can be changed through the will of the peoples of Northern Ireland. For practical purposes the legal sovereign is the constitution, while the political sovereign is the SACNI and the APNI.

(iv) Finally, there is an argument over whether the concept of sovereignty is historically outmoded, redundant or culturally parochial. Some maintain that the term is a leftover from the age of monarchs who owned lands and peoples, that its useful meanings can be conveyed just as well by notions like authority, power and responsibility, and that it is only a controversial notion in countries where legislatures possess unlimited right to make laws (as in the United Kingdom before it joined the European Community) and where there is no formal recognition of popular sovereignty. We sympathise with this viewpoint.

APPENDICES

B Rules for allocating chairs and committee seats in a Northern Ireland Assembly

B.1. There are two well known rules used for allocating seats in PR list systems which could be adapted for the purposes of filling committee chairships and committee places for the Assembly of the Peoples of Northern Ireland: the d'Hondt rule, and the Saint-Laguë rule.[45] Here we consider only the question of determining committee chairships.

B.2. To think about the possible outcomes of the two rules in deciding which parties obtain committee chairships consider the following example. Imagine that the Assembly for the Peoples of Northern Ireland has 100 members. Imagine that there are to be ten committees, and that therefore 10 committee chairs have to be found. Finally, imagine that after an election, in let us say 1996, the distribution of seats in the APNI is as follows:

Parties	Seats
Ulster Unionist Party (UUP)	30
Social Democratic and Labour Party (SDLP)	24
Democratic Unionist Party (DUP)	17
Sinn Féin (SF)	12
Alliance Party (AP)	9
Conservative Party (CON)	3
Democratic Left (DL)	1
Green Party (GP)	1
Independent Loyalists (IL)	2
Independent Nationalist (IN)	1

B.3. The d'Hondt and Saint-Laguë rules work by establishing a series of divisors. Each time a party receives a chair its seat total is divided by the appropriate divisor. The procedure for allocation follows an iterative process in which chairs are successively allocated to the party with the 'highest average' at each step.

B.4. *The d'Hondt rule.* The d'Hondt rule, which the UUP and the DUP say they favour for the Northern Ireland Assembly, uses successive divisors of 1, 2, 3, 4, ..., n. The 'average' (a) is defined as a party's seats (v) divided by the number of chairs (s) already allocated to it in the Assembly plus one: $a = V/(S + 1)$. The procedure for our example is demonstrated below. Each party's share of seats is listed in percent across the top, and the divisors $(S + 1)$ down the left hand side. The numbers in parentheses indicate chairs in the order allocated. The largest party, the UUP, gets the first chair, then its seat share is divided by two (one chair plus one). Now the second largest party, the SDLP, has the highest average and thus wins the second chair. The process continues until all 10 chairs have been filled.

So in this example, as the calculations in the next table show, chairs would be allocated as follows:
UUP: 3, SDLP: 3, DUP: 2, SF: 1, AP: 1.
The UUP would have the 1st, 4th and 7th choices of the 10 chairs available. The SDLP would have the 2nd, 6th and 10th choices, the DUP the 3rd and 9th choices, SF the 5th choice, and the AP the 8th choice.

S	S+1	UUP	SDLP	DUP	SF	AP	CON	DL	GP	IL	IN
0	1	30 (1)	24 (2)	17 (3)	12 (5)	9 (8)	3	1	1	2	1
1	2	15 (4)	12 (6)	8.5 (9)	6	4.5					
2	3	10 (7)	8 (10)	5.7	3						
3	4	7.5	3								

B.5. *The Saint-Laguë rule*. Whereas the d'Hondt rule uses divisors of 1, 2, 3, ... n, the Sainte-Laguë rule uses divisors of 1, 3, 5, ... n. The effect of these divisors is supposed to lessen considerably the relatively large party bonus inherent in the d'Hondt divisors, and to help the relatively smaller parties. The procedure for our example is demonstrated below. Each party's share of seats is listed in percent across the top, and the divisors down the left hand side. The numbers in parentheses indicate chairs in the order allocated. The largest party, the UUP, gets the first chair, then its seat share is divided by three. Now the second largest party, the SDLP, has the highest average and thus wins the second chair. The process continues until all 10 chairs have been filled.

divis-ors	UUP	SDLP	DUP	SF	AP	CON	DL	GP	IL	IN
1	30 (1)	24 (2)	17 (3)	12 (4)	9 (6)	3	1	1	2	1
3	10 (5)	8 (7)	5.7(9)	3	3					
5	6 (8)	4.8(10)								

So in this example, as the calculations in the table above show, chairs would be allocated as follows:
UUP: 3, SDLP: 3, DUP: 2, SF: 1, AP: 1.
The rule, in this example does not affect the overall number of chairs won by each party. However, in our example, the Sainte-Laguë rule would affect the rank-ordering in which parties would be able to choose committee chairships. The UUP would have the 1st, 5th and 8th choices, the SDLP the 2nd, 7th and 10th choices, the DUP the 3rd and 9th choices, SF the 4th choice, and the AP the 6th choice. In other words the biggest parties, the UUP and the SDLP would not win as many highly ranked chairs as under the d'Hondt rule, whereas some of the smaller parties, like SF and Alliance would get a better choice of prized chairs. In our example the DUP does marginally than under the d'Hondt rule.

Summary

B.6. The two rules do not, in this example, produce any differences in the number of chairs won by the parties. However, they do affect the rank-ordering

APPENDICES

in which parties win chairs. The smaller parties, the DUP, SF and the AP should rationally prefer the Saint-Laguë rule. Given that the smaller parties are less likely to be represented in the SACNI it seems reasonable to protect their interests in the Assembly by adopting the Saint-Laguë rule rather than the d'Hondt rule.

A Cautionary Note on Alliances and Coalitions

B.7. If parties are entitled, as they should be, to run alliances in the election for the APNI, or to form coalition parties within the assembly after the election, then this democratic possibility may appear to have serious implications for the rules governing committee-formation, and the rules governing the election of committee chairships. It is very likely that parties will behave strategically with regard to winning committee chairs or seats and consider forming coalitions to advance their ends. However, in our example there would only be very significant consequences if electoral alliances produced differences in the shares of seats won by unionists and nationalists in the APNI. Consider two possible scenarios of alliance or coalition formation.

B.7.1. In scenario (a) the UUP and DUP run a joint slate and win 47 seats in the 100 seat Assembly. All other parties retain the same share of seats. The allocation process under the d'Hondt rule would be as follows:

S	S+1	UUP-DUP		SDLP		SF		AP		CON	DL	GP	IL	IN
0	1	47	(1)	24	(2)	12	(5)	9	(9)	3	1	1	2	1
1	2	23.5	(3)	12	(6)	6		4.5						
2	3	15.7	(4)	8	(10)	4								
3	4	11.75	(7)	6										
4	5	9.4	(8)											
5	6	7.83												

So in this example chairs would be allocated as follows:
UUP-DUP: 5, SDLP: 3, SF: 1, AP: 1.

The UUP-DUP alliance would have the 1st, 3rd, 4th, 7th and 8th choice of chairs - the same as if the two parties ran without an alliance. In other words in this example the alliance between the UUP and DUP would not affect the overall unionist share or allocation of chairs. In fact no overall change occurs.

The Sainte-Laguë process, by contrast, would result in the following allocation of chairs in the table below. In other words it would produce the same overall allocation of chairs as under the d'Hondt rule (UUP-DUP: 5, SDLP: 3, SF: 1, AP: 1), but the rank-ordering of seats would be less favourable for the UUP-DUP alliance than under the d'Hondt rule (1st, 3rd, 5th, 8th and 9th compared with 1st, 3rd, 4t, 7th and 8th). The overall result is the same as that produced by Saint-Laguë with no UUP-DUP alliance. In this scenario while nationalists as a whole should prefer pure Saint-Laguë to the d'Hondt rule (because it worsens the rank-ordering of unionist chairs) the

SDLP may prefer the d'Hondt rule because they receive a better rank-ordering of chairs under d'Hondt, while SF receives a lower ranked chair.

divisors	UUP-DUP	SDLP	SF	AP	CON	DL	GP	IL	IN
1	47 (1)	24 (2)	12 (4)	9 (6)	3	1	1	2	1
3	15.7 (3)	8 (7)	4	3					
5	9.4 (5)	4.8 (10)							
7	6.7 (8)								
9	5.2 (9)								
11	4.3								

B.7.2. In scenario (b) the UUP-DUP alliance again wins 47 seats. However, this time its formation has consequences for the nationalist bloc. After abandoning its support for armed violence a reformed SF negotiates a joint programme with the SDLP and they jointly command a bloc of 36 seats in the Assembly. All other parties' share of seats won remains the same. The allocation of chairs under the d'Hondt rule would then be as follows:

S	S+1	UUP-DUP	SDLP-SF	AP	CON	DL	GP	IL	IN
0	1	47 (1)	36 (2)	9 (9)	3	1	1	2	1
1	2	23.5 (3)	18 (4)	4.5					
2	3	15.6 (5)	12 (6)						
3	4	11.75 (7)	9 (10)						
4	5	9.4 (8)							

In this scenario the outcome in terms of committee chairs would be
UUP-DUP: 5, SDLP-SF: 4, AP: 1.
This outcome is satisfactory from the perspective of proportionality (unionists with 47% of seats win 50% of chairs, nationalists with 36% of seats win 40% of chairs).

Under the Sainte-Laguë rule the allocation process would be as follows:

divisors	UUP-DUP	SDLP-SF	AP	CON	DL	GP	IL	IN
1	47 (1)	36 (2)	9 (6)	3	1	1	2	1
3	15.6 (3)	12 (4)	3					
5	9.4 (5)	7.2 (7)						
7	6.7 (8)	5.1 (10)						
9	5.2 (9)	4						
11	4.3							

The outcome in terms of committee chairs would be:
UUP-DUP: 5, SDLP-SF: 4, AP: 1.

Under Saint-Laguë the UUP-DUP alliance does less well in rank-ordering of chairs than under d'Hondt (it obtains the 1st, 3rd, 5th, 8th and 9th chairs compared with the 1st, 3rd, 5th, 7th, and 8th chairs). Under Saint-Laguë the nationalist alliance also does slightly less well (winning the 2nd, 4th, 7th and 10th choices, compared with 2nd, 4th, 6th and 10th). The AP does much better in rank-ordering under pure Saint-Laguë than under d'Hondt (winning the 6th rather than the 9th choice of chair).

B.8. In the above examples of possible coalition or alliance-formations the two rules are not very sensitive to the formation of alliances or coalitions. However, these examples have assumed, deliberately, that such alliances have no overall impact on the share of seats won by political parties. This assumption is unrealistic. Others things being equal, we would expect a unionist or nationalist alliance to increase the overall number of seats won by its constituent parties. Moreover, if one is pessimistic, at least in the short term, about the prospects of constitutionalising Sinn Féin there is good reason to believe that a unionist alliance is more likely to be formed than a nationalist alliance, and to believe that in such circumstances the d'Hondt rule would operate unfairly to the advantage of the unionist bloc, and to the disadvantage of the nationalist bloc and the Alliance Party.

B.9. Consider then the following scenario. An alliance is formed between the UUP and the DUP. It successfully squeezes the Conservative vote and the independent loyalist vote, while the SDLP and SF do not form an alliance and receive a slightly lower share of seats won than in the previous scenarios, leaking support to, say, Democratic Left and the Green Party. The number of seats held by parties in the APNI is now as follows: UUP-DUP: 50, SDLP: 23, SF: 11, AP: 9, Con: 1, DL: 2, GP: 2, Ind L: 1, Ind N: 1. Under the d'Hondt rule the allocation of committee chairs would proceed as follows:

S	S+1	UUP-DUP	SDLP	SF	AP	CON	DL	GP	IL	IN
0	1	50 (1)	23 (3)	11 (7)	9 (9)	1	2	2	1	1
1	2	25 (2)	11.5 (6)	5.5	4.5					
2	3	16.7 (4)	7.7							
3	4	12.5 (5)								
4	5	10 (8)								
5	6	8.3 (10)								
6	7	7.1								

In these circumstances the UUP-DUP alliance, with 50% of the seats, would take 6 or 60% of the committee chairs, with a very favourable rank-ordering (1st, 2nd, 4th, 5th, 8th and 10th choices). The nationalist bloc as a whole, with 35% of the seats, would take 3 committee chairs, with an unfavourable rank-ordering (3rd, 6th and 7th). The Alliance Party would obtain the 9th ranked committee chair.

B. 10. By contrast, consider what would occur under the Saint-Laguë when the allocation of committee chairs would proceed as indicated in the next table. In these circumstances the UUP-DUP alliance receives an exactly proportional share of the committee chairs (5), with a less favourable rank-ordering than under the d'Hondt rule (1st, 3rd, 5th, 8th and 9th choices). The nationalist bloc as a whole would now win 4 committee chairs with a much improved rank-ordering than under the d'Hondt rule (2nd, 4th, 7th and 10th). And the Alliance Party would win the 6th ranked committee chair.

divisors	UUP-DUP	SDLP	SF	AP	CON	DL	GP	IL	IN
1	50 (1)	23 (2)	11 (4)	9 (6)	1	2	2	1	1
3	16.7 (3)	7.7 (7)	3.7	3					
5	10 (5)	4.6 (10)							
7	7.1 (8)								
9	5.6 (9)								
11	4.5								

Why Saint-Laguë is better than d'Hondt

B.11. To sum up: in very plausible scenarios the d'Hondt rule may give a disproportional share of committee chairs and an unfairly favourable rank-ordering of chairs to the largest party, or the largest alliance. By contrast, the Sainte-Laguë rule ensures a reasonable share and ranking of chairs for the smaller parties, SF and the AP - and the DUP when it is not in alliance with the UUP, and when it does not perform well. We believe that there are good constitutional reasons, consistent with our model, to support a rule which is proportional, but which is not unduly generous to large parties (or coalitions) in the Assembly - especially as the small parties have lower probabilities of winning seats on the SACNI. To those concerned that the Saint-Laguë rule aids the DUP and SF too much we would point out, first, that any rule which benefits the Alliance Party is likely to benefit the DUP and SF, and secondly, that a successful constitutional model for Northern Ireland must be one which can be operated by the DUP and SF. We believe that the Saint-Laguë rule discussed here, or some variation on it *, fits best with our constitutional vision, and is a suitable rule for the allocation of committee chairs.

---

* A modified Saint-Laguë rule, employed in some Scandinavian systems, uses divisors of 1.4, 3, 5, ..., n. It functions to benefit middle-sized parties against small and large parties.

C The UK subvention of Northern Ireland, 1966-1993

Year (i)   Actual Prices £ millions   1992 Prices £ millions (iv)

	incl. security	excl. security	extra army costs	incl. security	excl. security	extra army costs
1967 (ii)	52	-	(iii)	489	-	-
1968 (ii)	63	-	(iii)	576	-	-
1969 (ii)	74	-	(iii)	644	-	-
1970 (ii)	74	-	2	612	-	17
1971 (ii)	88	-	7	673	-	54
1972 (ii)	126	-	14	883	-	98
1973 (ii)	181	-	29	1173	-	188
1974	312	292	33	1890	1769	200
1975	389	280	45	1969	1417	228
1976	565	413	60	2279	1666	242
1977	620	450	65	2202	1598	231
1978	688	515	69	2149	1609	216
1979	848	648	81	2389	1826	228
1980	944	695	96	2280	1678	232
1981	1090	781	111	2224	1594	226
1982	1064	716	149	1980	1332	277
1983	1149	783	143	1996	1360	248
1984	1305	921	141	2167	1529	234
1985	1489	1077	121	2353	1702	191
1986	1536	1087	135	2301	1629	202
1987	1593	1099	144	2312	1595	209
1988	1570	1010	166	2160	1390	228
1989	1698	1095	174	2178	1404	223
1999	1757	1095	201	2115	1318	242
1991	2018	1291	218	2249	1439	243
1992	2436	1620	317	2540	1689	330
1993 (v)	3296	2365	(v)	3296	2365	(vi)

Source: House of Commons Parliamentary Question, Hansard, 22 March 1993, col. 498

Notes
(i)   Year = Fiscal Year, e.g. 1967 = Fiscal Year 1966-67.
(ii)   Separate figures for security costs within subvention are available only from 1973-74. Until 1978-79 the costs shown were law and order costs borne on United Kingdom votes: from 1979-80 the costs are those of the Northern Ireland Office and the Northern Ireland Court Service.
(iii)   Figures for extra army costs are available only from 1969-70.
(iv)   Actual prices have been converted to 1992 prices by applying the appropriate Gross Domestic Product deflator.
(v)   Figures for 1992-93 are provisional.
(vi)   Figures for extra army costs for 1992-93 are not yet available.

D   Formulae for aid to Northern Ireland under shared authority

D.1. Under shared authority, security expenses would be directly paid for by the outside powers. In addition a financial subvention would be provided to the region, from which a special tax would be subtracted to meet part of the cost of security. The subvention, before and after the payment of this tax would be calculated according to formulae of the following type:

$$\text{GROSS-SUB} = r*(Y_{NI} - Y_{GB})*POP + F$$

$$\text{NET-SUB} = \text{GROSS-SUB} - t*SEC$$

where:

GROSS-SUB	=	Financial subvention *before* payment of security tax
NET-SUB	=	Financial subvention *after* payment of security tax
Y_{NI}, Y_{GB}	=	Gross domestic product *per capita* in NI and GB
POP	=	Population of Northern Ireland
SEC	=	Total expenditure by the outside powers on security relating to Northern Ireland
F	=	Fixed sum indexed to inflation
r	=	Income equalisation coefficient
t	=	Security tax coefficient

In these formulae:
- the term $r*(Y_{NI} - Y_{GB})*POP$ is an equalisation transfer designed to reduce the difference in *per capita* income levels in Northern Ireland and Great Britain;
- the term $t*SEC$ is the amount of security tax paid by NI;
- the term F is an indexed sum designed to ensure that NI does not lose out when the formulae are initially implemented.

D.2. As an illustration consider how the formulae would have been applied if implemented in the calendar year 1991. Suppose r = 0.4 and t = 0.4. *Per capita* GDP in NI and GB were £6567 and £8680 respectively in 1991. On a calendar basis the total cost of security relating to Northern Ireland in that year was an estimated £1,351million. (This estimate assumes that *per capita* expenditure on security by the Irish Republic is four times large as that of Great Britain.) On a calendar basis the actual subvention to Northern Ireland, excluding security, was an estimated £1,538 million in 1991. Using the assumed coefficients, this figure for the non-security component can be derived from our formulae as follows in the calculations in the next table. The fixed sum (£(UK) 731 million) is designed to ensure that the ultimate amount of financial aid in 1991 is equal to the subvention (excluding security) actually received in that year.

APPENDICES

	£ (UK) millions
Income equalisation transfer	1,347
plus	
Fixed sum	731
equals	
Gross-sub financial aid	2,068
minus	
Security 'tax'	-540
equals	
Net-financial aid	1,538

D.3. The parameters used in this example have the following implications for the value of the subvention in future years. For every £(UK) 100 reduction in *per capita* GDP in Northern Ireland (as compared to *per capita* GDP in Great Britain), the amount of financial aid is increased by £(UK)40. For every £(UK) 100 reduction in security expenditure relating to NI the amount of security tax paid by Northern Ireland is reduced by £(UK) 40. Thus, under our formulae, the subvention helps to compensate for differences in *per capita* income between Northern Ireland and Great Britain. It also ensures that a significant part of any savings in security expenditure are passed on to the population of Northern Ireland. The formulae work in the opposite direction if the region starts to catch up economically with Great Britain, or if security expenditure rises.

D.4. Note that our formulae would have to be modified if the gap in income levels between Northern Ireland and Great Britain were to close significantly and if peace led to a convergence between levels of security expenditure in the two areas. In these circumstances, the fixed part F would have to be phased out. Otherwise, an anomalous situation would arise in which the subvention was used to provide an average standard of living in Northern Ireland higher than in the prime donor country, Great Britain - hardly an acceptable outcome to British taxpayers.

E Comparative statistics on the economies of Northern Ireland, the Republic of Ireland and Great Britain, 1990

	Northern Ireland	Irish Republic	Great Britain
Population (millions)	1.6	3.5	55.8
Gross National Product			
Total (£ (UK) billion)	(1) 10.1	17.5	(2) 471.4
Per Capita £ (UK)	6360	4992	8445
Personal Consumption			
Per Capita £ (UK)	5131	3645	6131
Public Services (3)			
Per capita £ (UK)	2177	1289	1594
Unemployment (%) (4)	17.1	14.2	6.6

Sources: OECD *National Accounts*
 CSO *Regional Trends*
 OECD *Main Economic Indicators*

Notes:
(1) Gross Domestic Product.
(2) Includes continental shelf.
(3) 'Public Services' covers total public expenditure excluding defence, debt-interest, social security, agriculture and business subsidies. In Northern Ireland, those costs of law and order associated with political violence are excluded. The figures shown here are from data in the Cadogan Group *Northern Limits* (Belfast, 1992), op. cit. p. 33.
(4) Figures based on the EC Labour Force Sample Survey.

F Composition of Gross National Product, Northern Ireland & Great Britain, 1990 (£ per capita)

	Northern Ireland	Great Britain	NI/GB
Agriculture	276	149	1.85
Industry (1)	1977	(2) 2933	0.67
Public Administration and Defence	859	542	1.58
Health and Education	885	778	1.14
Other services (3)	2364	4000	0.59
Gross Domestic Product	6360	8408	0.76
Interest, profits and dividends from outside (net)	(4) n.a.	38	n.a.
Gross National Product	6360	8445	0.75

Sources: CSO *Regional Trends*, CSO, *Blue Book*

Notes:
(1) Energy and Water, Manufacturing, Construction.
(2) Includes continental shelf.
(3) Includes ownership of dwellings and adjustments for financial services.
(4) Probably small.

G Main flows of income into Northern Ireland, 1990

	£ (UK) million	%
Exports of Goods	4125	60
Tourism and other Services	450	6
Private Sector Investment	400	6
Subvention	<u>1952</u>	<u>28</u>
Total	6927	100

Source: Cadogan Group *Northern Limits* (Belfast, 1992), p. 32. The subvention has been converted from a fiscal year to a calendar year basis.

Note: The value of exports includes direct imports purchased to produce exports. The other items in the table above also include some direct imports, but to a lesser extent than for exports. Calculations excluding direct imports would thus show the subvention to be even more important.

NOTES

1 Interview with Brendan O'Leary, broadcast on Analysis, BBC Radio 4: November 26 1992.

2 The most extensive analytical catalogue of the rival understandings is contained in John Whyte's *Interpreting Northern Ireland* (Oxford: Oxford University Press, 1990). See also Brendan O'Leary and John McGarry *The Politics of Antagonism: Understanding Northern Ireland* (London: Athlone, 1993) and John McGarry and Brendan O'Leary *Explaining Northern Ireland: Broken Images* (Oxford: Basil Blackwell, forthcoming).

3 See Michael Laffan's *The Partition of Ireland* (Dundalk: Dundalgan Press, 1983) and O'Leary and McGarry *The Politics of Antagonism* op.cit. (1993: Chapters 2 and 3).

4 The definitive study is David Smith's and Gerald Chambers's *Inequality in Northern Ireland* (Oxford: Oxford University Press, 1991). See also R. Cormack and R.D. Osborne (eds.) *Discrimination and Public Policy in Northern Ireland* (Oxford: Oxford University Press, 1991).

5 For further discussion and comparisons see O'Leary and McGarry *The Politics of Antagonism* op.cit. (1993: Chapter 1).

6 Instead of elaborating how to address material and unjustified inequalities we can simply state that we support the detailed proposals for social and economic reform made in 1988 by the Labour front bench - see K. McNamara, J. Marshall and M. Mowlam *Towards a United Ireland. Reform and Harmonisation: A Dual Strategy for Irish Unification* (London: 1988).

7 For further discussion of constitutional failures in Northern Ireland see Christopher McCrudden 'Northern Ireland and the British Constitution' in J. Jowell and D. Oliver (eds.) *The Changing Constitution* (2nd edition), (Oxford: Oxford University Press) and B.O'Leary and J. McGarry *The Politics of Antagonism* (op. cit.) Chapters 3 and 4.

8 Here and below we follow Arend Lijphart *Democracies: Patterns of Majoritarian and Consensus Government in Twenty-One Countries* (New Haven: Yale University Press, 1984), Chapter 1.

9 A. Lijphart, *Democracy in Plural Societies* (New Haven: Yale University Press, 1977).

10 Here and below we draw upon the works of R. Dahl, *A Preface to Democratic Theory* (Chicago: Chicago University Press, 1956) and M.J.C. Vile *Constitutionalism and the Separation of Powers* (Oxford: Oxford University Press, 1967).

11   See R. Dahl *Polyarchy: Participation and Opposition* (New Haven: Yale University Press, 1971).

12   See B. O'Leary, 'Public Opinion and Northern Irish Futures', *Political Quarterly,* 1992, 63, 2: 143-70, especially Table 5.

13   See Chapter 6.

14   In these respects (power-sharing, proportionality, community autonomy and constitutional safeguards) our proposals are consociational - as elaborated by the Dutch political scientist Arend Lijphart in his book *Democracy in Plural Societies* (New Haven: Yale University Press, 1977). However, our proposals are elaborated within a framework of shared authority, and unlike Lijphart we believe that consociation can work with a separation of powers, including a multi-person presidency (see Chapter 3). Lijphart's opposition to presidentialism has been based on the idea that it is necessarily majoritarian, but that is so only if presidentialism requires a single president. In his Stein Rokkan lecture in Leiden Lijphart seemed to envisage the possibility of reconciling presidentialism and proportionalism (April 4 1993).

15   Martin Dent 'The Feasibility of Shared Sovereignty (and Shared Authority)' in Charles Townshend (ed.) *Consensus in Ireland* (Oxford: Clarendon Press, 1988), p. 130.

16   F.W. Boal and J.N.H. Douglas commended the logic of joint authority suggested by T.J. Pickvance in their edited collection *Integration and Division: Geographical Perspectives on the Northern Ireland Problem* (London: Academic Press), pp. 355-56. Basil Chubb argues that 'the first steps down the road that could lead to a condominium' have already been taken, and clearly believes that it is a better idea than the notions put forward by 'the protagonist of both communities [engaged in] the futile pursuit of unattainable objectives' -*The Politics of the Irish Constitution* (Dublin: Institute of Public Administration), pp. 95, 94. He thinks of joint authority as a long-run venture, and argues that both communities will require considerable powers of self-government within a framework of 'tripartite institutions.' Bernard Cullen and Richard Kearney made a joint submission in favour of joint sovereignty to the New Ireland Forum. However, neither of these philosophers appears presently to support the idea. Desmond Fennell has argued in favour of joint authority on several occasions, influencing the climate of opinion which led the SDLP to advocate the idea of a condominium in 1972 (see *inter alia* his chapter entitled 'Facts for Peace in the North' in *The State of the Nation: Ireland Since the 1960s* (Dublin, Ward River Press, 1983)). The late John Whyte wrote favourably of joint authority in his posthumously published *Interpreting Northern Ireland*, whilst recognising the difficulties it might produce. He did not however, endorse it, and indeed endorsed no proposal (Whyte, op.cit., pp. 238-242). The late Frank Wright's arguments were

best made in his lucid article 'Northern Ireland and the British-Irish Relationship' *Studies: An Irish Quarterly Review* , 1989, 78, 310: 151-62.

17   Bernard Crick's criticisms of the doctrine of parliamentary sovereignty and its implications for Northern Ireland are developed in 'The Sovereignty of Parliament and the Irish Question' in Desmond Rea (ed.) *Political Co-operation in Divided Societies* (Dublin, Gill and Macmillan, 1982), pp. 229-54. Martin Dent's case is elaborated in 'The Feasibility of Shared Sovereignty (and Shared Authority' in Charles Townshend (ed.) *Consensus in Ireland* (Oxford, Clarendon Press, 1988), pp. 128-56. T.J. Pickvance's pamphlet, *The Northern Ireland Problem: Peace with Equity* (Birmingham, 1975) was partly derived from his experience on a commission which investigated the Austrian and Italian conflict over the South Tyrol. The Kilbrandon Committee, an independent British response to the New Ireland Forum, made its argument in a document published under the title *Report of an Independent Inquiry 'To Consider the Report of the New Ireland Forum, Examine the Practicality of any Proposals Made in the Report by Any Other Sources, and Make Recommendations'* (London, 1984). Arguments about joint authority are fairly reviewed by the philosopher Anthony Kenny in his chapter 'Joint Authority' published in John McGarry and Brendan O'Leary (eds) *The Future of Northern Ireland* (Oxford: Clarendon Press, 1990), pp. 219-41.

18   A. Pollak (ed.) *A Citizens' Inquiry* (Dublin, 1993), p. 162. Given that the first and second most popular submissions were for a devolved government within the UK (first) and for a united Ireland (second) evidently shared authority is the median political proposal.

19   New Ireland Forum *Report* (Stationery Office, Dublin, 1984), 8.7., p. 38.

20   See Brendan O'Leary 'Public Opinion and Northern Irish Futures' *Political Quarterly,* 1992, 63, 2: 143-70.

21   No member representing an Irish constituency voted for the third reading of the Government of Ireland Bill (Hansard, Vol. 134, 11 November 1920, cols. 1464-1466] - as a check against Dod's Parliamentary Companion for the relevant period confirms (Our thanks to L. Cooper of the Reference Services Section of the House of Commons Library).

22   For more detailed discussions see *inter alia* Michael Laffan *The Partition of Ireland, 1911-1925* (Dundalk, 1983), O'Leary and McGarry *The Politics of Antagonism* (op. cit.), chs. 2-3, and John McGarry and Brendan O'Leary *Explaining Northern Ireland: Broken Images* (Oxford, Basil Blackwell: forthcoming), ch.1.

23   See O'Leary 'Public Opinion and Northern Irish Futures' op.cit. (1992) p. 154. The option most closely resembling shared authority referred to 'a devolved government jointly guaranteed by and responsible to the British and Irish governments'.

24 We accept the merits of Joe Ruane's and Jennifer Todd's arguments that so far the nationalist demand for equality has been incompatible with unionists' need for security - and that this tension structures much of the antagonism in Northern Ireland (see J. Ruane and J. Todd "Why can't you get along with each other?' Culture, structure and the Northern Ireland conflict' in Eamonn Hughes (ed.) *Culture and Politics in Northern Ireland* (Buckingham, Open University Press, 1991), pp. 27-44. Shared authority offers the best way of transcending this tension.

25 For discussions of the weaknesses of the Northern Ireland economy see *inter alia* R. Rowthorn and N. Wayne, *Northern Ireland: The Political Economy of Conflict* (Oxford: Polity Press, 1988), P. Teague (ed.) *The Northern Ireland Economy* (London: Lawrence and Wishart, 1993), P. Teague (ed.) *Beyond the Rhetoric: Politics, the Economy and Social Policy in Northern Ireland* (London: Lawrence and Wishart, 1987) (especially the essays by B. Rowthorn, B. Moore and P. Canning), the Cadogan Group *Northern Limits* (Belfast, 1992), op.cit., and F. Gaffikin and M. Morrisey, *Northern Ireland: The Thatcher Years* (London: Zed Press, 1990).

26 See Smith and Chambers *Inequality in Northern Ireland* (Oxford: 1991) op. cit.

27 For a more detailed discussion of this point see Rowthorn and Wayne *Northern Ireland* (Oxford: 1988) op. cit. and the Cadogan Group *Northern Limits* (Belfast: 1992), op. cit. The need for external aid for the Northern Ireland economy was earlier stressed in a report written by DKM consultants for the New Ireland Forum, *The macroeconomic consequences of integrated economic policy, planning and co-ordination in Ireland*, (Dublin: Stationery Office, 1984).

28 This chapter draws heavily upon O'Leary and McGarry *The Politics of Antagonism* (1993, Chapter 8), op. cit.

29 B. O'Leary, 'Public Opinion and Northern Ireland Futures' *Political Quarterly*, op.cit. Figure 2.

30 We accept that there are grounds for scepticism about such poll-findings - see the note accompanying paragraph 2.5 above.

31 See Rowthorn and Wayne *Northern Ireland* (1988 op. cit.) p. 209, or O'Leary and McGarry *The Politics of Antagonism* (1993) op.cit. p. 131.

32 See O'Leary and McGarry *The Politics of Antagonism* (1993) op.cit. pp. 185-93.

33 See K. McNamara, J. Marshall, and M. Mowlam *Towards a United Ireland. Reform and Harmonisation: A Dual Strategy for Irish*

Unification (London: 1988) and Rowthorn and Wayne *Northern Ireland* (1988) op.cit.

34 Liam de Paor *Unfinished Business: Ireland Today and Tomorrow* (Dublin, 1990) p. 158.

35 L. Kennedy *Two Ulsters: A case for repartition* (Belfast, 1986) and see also his chapter 'Repartition' in McGarry and O'Leary (eds.) *The Future of Northern Ireland* (1990), op.cit. pp. 137-61.

36 Interview with B. O'Leary, 3.1.1991.

37 Martin Smyth, *A Federated People* (Belfast, 1987).

38 See John Whyte, *Interpreting Northern Ireland,* op.cit. (1990), p. 241.

39 See John McGarry and Brendan O'Leary (eds.) *The Politics of Ethnic Conflict Regulation* (London: Routledge, 1993: Chapter 1).

40 Interview with B.O'Leary, 3.1.1991.

41 See D. Fennell 'Facts for Peace in the North' in *The State of the Nation: Ireland Since the 1960s* (Dublin, Ward River Press, 1983). Since he wrote pieces advocating transitional joint sovereignty for the *Irish Press* in 1971 Fennell has since elaborated arguments which are consistent with our conception of a durable model of shared authority. See D. Fennell *Beyond Nationalism: The Struggle Against Provinciality in the Modern World* (Swords: 1985) and *The Revision of Irish Nationalism* (Dublin: 1989).

42 See the SDLP's document *Towards a New Ireland* (Belfast, 1972).

43 See the summary of Michael Farrell's submission in A. Pollak (ed.) *A Citizens' Inquiry: The Opsahl Report on Northern Ireland* (Dublin: 1993).

44 P. King 'Sovereignty', in Miller, D., Coleman, W. and Ryan, A. (eds.) *The Blackwell Encyclopaedia of Political Thought* (Oxford: Basil Blackwell, 1991), pp. 492-5.

45 See R. Taagepera and M.S. Shugart *Seats and Votes: The Effects and Determinants of Electoral Systems* (New Haven, Yale University Press, 1989), especially pp. 19-37.